The Robust City

Cities expand, upwards and outwards, and their physical structure can last a very long time, not just tens but hundreds of years. Nevertheless, they are rarely designed for expansion. Their layout does not allow for extension or for the retrofitting of infrastructure and can constrain, and often prevent, the growth and change of activities within them – cities are not 'robust' in their design. In other words, change is not planned for but involves costly reconstruction.

The Robust City argues that a robust, expandable and sustainable urban form can be deduced from planning goals. Development should not just follow public transport corridors but should not be allowed beyond walking distance from them. This would create 'green enclaves' that would permit not only recreational access but also the retrofitting of infrastructure and the efficient circulation of motor vehicles. The same principles could also be applied within neighbourhoods to facilitate the rational handling of urban intensification.

Tony Hall is an Adjunct Professor within the Urban Research Program at Griffith University, Brisbane, Australia. Since his move to Australia in 2004, he has published a number of significant works on sustainable urban form, including his 2010 book on the demise of the Australian backyard which won the PIA national award for cutting-edge research in 2012.

He was previously Professor of Town Planning at Anglia Ruskin University, Chelmsford, UK. A specialist originally in transport planning and later in urban design, his 30-year academic career in Britain produced notable publications in the field of design guidance. Rather unusually, he also served as a local councillor and led the City of Chelmsford's planning policy for seven years. He was instrumental in raising the general standards of design resulting in a government award to the city for the quality of the built environment in 2003.

Routledge Research in Planning and Urban Design
Series editor: Peter Ache
Radboud University, Nijmegen, Netherlands

Routledge Research in Planning and Urban Design is a series of academic monographs for scholars working in these disciplines and the overlaps between them. Building on Routledge's history of academic rigour and cutting-edge research, the series contributes to the rapidly expanding literature in all areas of planning and urban design.

The Robust City

Tony Hall

Routledge
Taylor & Francis Group

LONDON AND NEW YORK

First published 2015
by Routledge
2 Park Square, Milton Park, Abingdon, Oxfordshire OX14 4RN

and by Routledge
711 Third Avenue, New York, NY 10017

First issued in paperback 2016

*Routledge is an imprint of the Taylor & Francis Group, an informa
business*

British Library Cataloguing in Publication Data
A catalogue record for this book is available from the British Library

Library of Congress Cataloging in Publication Data
A catalog record for this book has been requested

ISBN: 978-1-138-63140-3 (pbk)
ISBN: 978-1-138-80132-5 (hbk)

Typeset in Sabon
by HWA Text and Data Management, London

Contents

Figures and tables

Figures

Tables

Preface

The development of the original themes on which this book is based goes back some way. I first started to bring them together at the end of the 1990s and presented them as papers to conferences from 2003 onwards. Other projects then had to take precedence and I was able to return to them only in 2010. This book enabled me for the first time to set out my ideas as a complete argument and to assemble them into what, hopefully, readers will find to be a coherent whole. The approach could be seen as a neo-rational one in that it deduces desired city form from societal goals. However, there is an important difference from previous rational models. It is principles for guiding long-term physical form that are deduced, not human activities within the city. The argument could be seen as making the case for planning in general – the need for a planned city and what it would look like.

It follows, as a reflection on this argument, that most modern cities are not planned at all, at least in terms of the large-scale, long-term picture. Where planning regimes are strongest, the beneficial effects can largely be confined to the small scale and the shorter term. This is not to say that these are unimportant – they certainly are not – but that some of the principal purposes of planning can be neglected and forgotten.

What this book does not do is examine examples across the world to build up evidence of this failing. This could be done but would take at least one, more likely several, other books to do it and the message would be largely a negative one. The task of this book is to make positive practical proposals: to show how cities could be planned rather than concentrate on their shortcomings. This leads on to the question of how these proposals could be implemented. This is something that would have to be achieved through local political processes and this is also a very important matter. The lack of large-scale, long-term planning arises from the failure to confront the many challenges within these very same processes. However, to address this issue properly would also require at least one, more likely several, additional books. This book should be seen, therefore, as the starting point in the process. To succeed in political argument and campaigning it is necessary to have something to aim at. This book seeks to provide a target that is clear, tangible and practical. It shows how cities could be planned such that they could be made robust in the long term.

Introduction

The argument of this book is that settlements and patterns of settlements should be so designed that, as circumstances change, they need the minimum of alteration to their existing form in order to accommodate changes of use, increases in intensity of use and expansion in size. This arises from the perception that the physical structure of a settlement lasts longer than the uses to which it is put. Moreover, the period over which it endures is from 60 to many hundreds of years. It is not suggested that the physical form does not change incrementally but, rather, that elements of it may change at different rates with some changing not at all. For example, buildings may be refurbished or replaced but the outlines of the plot and street may remain.

The idea that buildings should be designed to be capable of being reused, adapted and extended is, hopefully, a fairly well established design principle, if not one necessarily reflected in what actually gets built. It is taken further here as a principle that should apply not just to buildings but to the street layout, to the design of whole towns and cities and to how urban areas relate to each other within city regions. It is argued that planning should provide a long-term physical context within which other short-term matters are played out. The efficiency of this physical context would be judged by how 'robust' it was and how little it needed to be changed in the long term.

The importance of this idea is reinforced by the observation that, in the modern world, settlements tend to multiply and to expand. Even though, in the short term, parts of cities and smaller settlements may exhibit decline, or even abandonment, contraction over a wide area, say a whole city-region, is very rare in the long term. This expansion not only creates new physical form but also places a burden on the existing urban fabric, particularly its infrastructure. This creates pressure for reconstruction as, unfortunately, the existing infrastructure is rarely designed to cope with the overall expansion of the city. If it had been so planned, then subsequent development costs and disruption to the inhabitants could be reduced. This is what the planned city should be about.

It will be argued that it is possible to derive the design of robust physical form at all scales, from city regions to the local level, from two sets of goals – pursuit of quality of life and pursuit of sustainability. At first sight, this might appear an outrageously ambitious claim but what is remarkable is that such a deduction results in planning ideas that are already familiar. What is new is the understanding of the way they can be put on a comprehensive and rational basis. At the more strategic level, there is the principle of development being concentrated within walking distance of a stop on a high-quality public transport route. At the more local level, there are the principles common in urban design practice in both many European countries and in American New Urbanism regarding active, pedestrian-scale streets lined with low-rise buildings incorporating natural light and ventilation and access to green space. All of these can be put on the same rational and systematic basis.

The next step in the argument offers this book's most original contribution. The robust and sustainable form derived from the goals becomes the only development allowed and the principle of 'transit-oriented development' is taken to its logical conclusion. This generates a new theoretical model for the city and city region and this model is found to have some remarkable properties. It provides a high level of accessibility for both public and private transport. It provides compact urban development combined with access to undeveloped 'green' areas throughout. It permits retrofitting of infrastructure with minimum disruption as the city expands. Moreover, all this can be achieved without necessarily relying on a physical master plan but through a set of principles governing spatial location. These principles can form the basis for the proper and effective planning of the expansion of existing cities and also for their urban intensification.

The structure of the book

The first chapter makes the important, but rarely fully appreciated, point that the structure of urban form persists over very long time periods, in contrast to land-use activities which change much more rapidly. It goes to make a second rarely appreciated point that urban form can constrain activities even when it cannot promote them. All decisions affecting the physical form of urban areas have, therefore, very long-term effects and great importance should be attached to them.

The second chapter addresses the implications of the use of the motor vehicle for the design of urban form. Although there are important energy and pollution issues associated with motor vehicles, the ultimate problem is the space they take up, something that can be partially reduced through maintenance of lower speeds. The operation of the motor vehicle is intimately linked, at all speed levels, with the design of physical form.

Chapter 3 argues that it is unwise to assume that the expansion of cities is not inevitable. Cities must, therefore, be designed to be extended but, unfortunately, this has almost never been the case in practice. Peripheral extensions have usually rounded-off urban areas rather than providing connections to enable them to be extended further. The continual growth of cities, both outward and upward, also requires expensive retrofitting of the existing urban form which has not be designed to facilitate expansion. Urban areas should, instead, be designed to make them 'robust', which makes them capable of both expansion and being retrofitted with minimum disturbance, over time.

How then to design a robust urban form? Chapter 4 argues that the qualities advocated by contemporary urban design practice and criteria for the sustainable location of development can be deduced logically from the goals of pursuit of sustainability and quality of life. These qualities are already familiar from current progressive planning theory and practice. The point that is made is that by being deduced from planning goals they can be put on a logical and rational basis.

Chapter 5 takes these locational criteria and design qualities and shows how they lead to specific typologies for buildings and streets, in particular perimeter blocks, shallow-plan buildings, a mix of uses and walkable neighbourhoods. Again, these are all familiar ideas from current progressive planning theory and practice but here they are put on a rational basis and into a logical context. What is novel is a proposal for a road hierarchy with only two levels: 'frontage with low speeds' and 'no active frontage'.

Chapter 6 begins the construction of a theoretical model of the 'robust city' demonstrating that:

- the locational criteria developed in Chapter 4 lead to 'ped-sheds' where development is restricted to within walking distance around stations on quality public transport networks;
- this also provides walking access to green space around the ped-sheds;
- residential density can be variable both within and between ped-sheds;
- some ped-sheds can be primarily non-residential, providing, for example, for park-and-ride, distribution and manufacturing facilities.

The result is what is often called a 'beads on a string' form. While there is nothing essentially new in this as a general approach, what is novel is an insistence on a prohibition of major development outside the 'ped-sheds' and the creation of separate non-residential 'ped-sheds' for park-and-ride and low-intensity public and commercial facilities. The chapter discusses the relationship of these ideas to 'neighbourhood' theory and practice over time.

In Chapter 7 the 'beads on a string' form is used to create a theoretical model for a whole city. An original arrangement using branching public transport lines is employed. This model is found to have some remarkable properties:

- it can be extended indefinitely while maintaining sustainability and quality of life;
- it creates large 'non-built-up' areas with the city;
- it allows for the retrofitting of infrastructure;

- it is completely accessible by either walking or public transport plus walking;
- it provides for the unimpeded circulation of motor vehicles outside residential areas.

Comparisons with examples from theory and practice, past and present, are then discussed. Although there are many points of partial correspondence, both the model as a whole and its particular implications for planning are shown to be entirely new.

Opportunities for constructing complete new cities based on the theoretical model will be very limited. Nevertheless, Chapter 8 argues that the combination of both the theoretical model and the typology of urban form developed in Chapter 5 can have practical application to the design of urban extensions and the intensification of existing urban areas. In particular, the approach derived from the theoretical model could provide a practical 'formula' for the systematic planning of extensions and intensification. The longer-term physical planning of urban extensions and the intensification of existing urban areas would be based on locational criteria rather than detailed master plans. The advantages this brings are two-fold: the location of new development is placed on a firmly rational basis and the new urban form will be able to respond flexibly to changes in residential density over time.

The implications for development plans and other statements of planning policy are addressed by Chapter 9. It argues that structuring development plans on the prescription of urban form, rather than predominantly on land-use activities, can be advantageous and that such plans can deal with incremental change in urban forms.

1 The persistence of form

The first point that needs to be clearly established is that the physical form of urban areas lasts a very long time. Dwellings may, typically, have a design life of 60 years or so but the reality is usually longer and this period is probably lengthening. In Europe, North America and many other parts of the world, dwellings constructed in the latter half of the nineteenth century are still in use today in large numbers. Some urban areas in Europe and the Americas contain significant urban fabric dating from the eighteenth century or even earlier. Refurbishment, repair and extension keep these buildings in use. They may change in use and intensity of use, but they retain their basic structure. Some commercial and industrial buildings may, indeed, have a design life of less than 50 years but there are also many others that are retained for very much longer. Some that have survived from the late nineteenth century, such as large textile mills, may now be retained in perpetuity even though their original use has vanished and may never return. Conservation polices, although comparatively recent arrivals in the historical context, show no sign of going out of fashion. As their influence becomes more and more significant, the point has now been reached where if a major building survives beyond its initially planned period of use, it is likely to be retained and conserved rather than be demolished. As new buildings of quality are constructed, so the absolute number of conserved structures will increase and, in some cases, the proportion of total buildings that is conserved may increase also.

The same arguments can be applied to transport infrastructure. Major roads may sometimes be widened out of all recognition but the historic line of route usually remains. Whereas urban motorways are clear examples of new construction that paid little or no heed to the existing patterns of urban form, they are rarely removed. Where this has happened, as for example in Portland, Oregon, Boston, Massachusetts, and San Francisco, California, in the US and Seoul in Korea, the policy has been to create public open space along the line of route rather than build over the space created, so retaining the original alignment. Similarly, although many of the urban areas created by nineteenth century industry may have lost the majority of their railways, those railway rights of way that survived into the late twentieth century show no signs of disappearing in the twenty-first. Whether converted to a recreational footpath, or where the railway has been retained and modernised, their routes remain an essential part of the contemporary city. Canals have proved even more difficult to remove. Birmingham in England is a notable example. Looking at the important recreational and amenity role played by its canal network nowadays it may be surprising to hear that it was the city council's policy in the 1950s and 1960s to remove them as outdated industrial relics. However, it was discovered that they also formed an integral part of the city's water supply system and their removal would have been impractical and costly. This is not just true for canals but also for docks and other port facilities. In port cities throughout the world, as new ports are created downstream or out of town, the old ones may be redeveloped for residential use but their waterways are rarely filled in.

Degrees of persistence

Academic studies that support these general observations can be found within the field of inquiry of *urban morphology*. The purpose of this book is not to describe this subject as such, as this is done very competently elsewhere, but to draw upon some of its insights into the historic evolution of urban form. In particular, studies in urban morphology have drawn attention to the persistence, that is, the survival over very long time periods, of particular aspects of urban form. Generally, town plans and street patterns exhibit a high degree of persistence both for the reasons set out above and also because the legal process of transfer of ownership tends to preserve the boundaries of a landholding long after the original use may have disappeared.

Within urban morphology, it is the work of Conzen that is of most relevance to the argument here. Not only did he develop his own conceptual structure within geography, drawing upon a German tradition going back to the latter part of the nineteenth century, but he carried out both academic research on town and country planning and was involved in planning practice. This diverse experience led eventually to his significant study of Alnwick, Northumberland (Conzen, 1960). In this book, Conzen analysed the historic development of the town plan of Alnwick from ancient times through to the mid-twentieth century. His conceptual structure focused upon *buildings* in their *plots* and how they were *contained* within *streets* and *blocks*. He observed that the rate of growth outwards from the historic core showed discontinuities over time resulting in the formation of *fringe belts*. Within these belts the built form displayed a morphological cohesion relating to the mode of origin although incorporating a variety of land uses. His analysis also permitted the recording and understanding of how, over time, types of urban form emerged from within a structure laid down by their predecessors. This process was often accompanied by the persistence of older boundary lines as a result of the constraints of the legal process of conveying land ownership. During the 1980s he developed his ideas further. By means of a study of Ludlow, Shropshire (Conzen, 1988), he refined his method, making more explicit the different degrees of persistence of town plan, building fabric and land use, which he termed *systematic form complexes*. His findings, shown by Table 1.1, were that the town plan, the outlines of the principal street system, plot pattern and building arrangements, had remained substantially unchanged over a 1000-year period. There had, of course, been more minor changes both to them and also to the building fabric in different periods but, even for the building fabric, a considerable proportion of it had been retained. On the other hand, he observed that land utilisation showed minimal persistence.

This brings us to an issue of terminology. Conzen refers to *land utilisation* by which is meant residential, business, recreation and similar uses. It is common in contemporary planning policy to use the term *land use* to represent a type of activity that is distinct from the land and structures that accommodates it. On the other hand, some structures are effectively defined by their use, notably transport facilities. A road or railway when no longer used is termed a *disused road* or *disused railway*; it does not lose its land-use name. To minimise any semantic confusion, this discussion will try to maintain a distinction between *built form* and the human *activities* associated with it. When the term *land use* is used it will also be in the sense of human activities such as living (residential), working (employment), recreation and so on, rather than the physical structures associated with them.

It is true that some areas of cities have undergone, and are still subject to, reconstruction that obliterates all records of the original form. Hausmann's rebuilding of central Paris in the nineteenth century and the rebuilding in the 1960s of parts of city centres and inner-city areas in most developed countries, particularly those associated with housing renewal, are well-known examples. However, in both historic perspective and geographical extent, these events have proved uncommon, if only because of the financial and legal obstacles that have stood in their way. In some cases, where such comprehensive redevelopment has taken place, particularly in the reconstruction of central and inner-city areas during the 1960s, the later structures were subsequently demolished and elements of the original street pattern restored. For example, the Bullring in the centre of Birmingham in England was a nineteenth-century market on a site going back to far earlier times. In the early 1960s it was covered by a very large indoor shopping centre that obliterated all traces of the original street pattern. This was itself demolished in the late 1990s and the new shopping centre that replaced it restored the vistas along the lines of the original main roads.

It is also worth noting that public parks enjoy a very high level of persistence. This may seem a rather obvious point but it is nonetheless significant for it. The same is not, however, true of sports fields, including those owned by schools and universities (which are not strictly public if not entirely private) and these may often end up being redeveloped and built over.

Table 1.1 Conzen's systematic form complexes for Ludlow with degrees of persistence

1	2	3	4	Contribution to hierarchy of townscape regions
Systematic form complex	Degree of form persistence	Morphological periods	Morphological constituents of historical stratification	
Town plan	Maximal	High medieval 1090–1220	General outlines of street system, plot pattern and building arrangement	High rank (major genetic plan units), intermediate rank (neighbourhoods: street and precinctual units, high medieval suburbs)
		Late medieval 1270–1500 and early post-medieval	Major island and lateral encroachments on street market, ubiquitous changes to street lines by minor lateral encroachments, ubiquitous minor alterations to plot pattern	Intermediate rank (Eastern Dinham transformation, Bell Lane, neighbourhood), lowest rank (morphotopes of market encroachment)
Building fabric	Considerable though varying with periods	High and late medieval 1090–1500	Few but prominent public buildings and defence structures. Very few houses by external indices, but structural remains inside and at rear of many post-medieval houses	
		Early modern 1500–1840	Majority of houses in localised period mixtures	Intermediate rank, but principally lowest rank (morphotopes)
		Victorian and Edwardian 1840–1918	Houses in peripheral location or on minor streets. A few commercial buildings in business core	Lowest rank (morphotopes)
		Inter-war and post war, post-1918	Very few buildings within Old Town	
Urban land utilisation		Pre-1840	Major land use area (business core, residential areas, institutional precincts)	Intermediate rank (traditional business core, traditional residential area, recreational area, castle ruins)
	Minimal	Recent (twentieth century)		

Source: Conzen, 1988.

If the physical form of towns and cities exhibits a high degree of persistence over time, what then does change? As Conzen observed, it is the land uses, in the sense of the human activities on and within the urban form. In general, land uses change at a faster rate than physical form. Not all land uses change but, where change occurs, it can be significant. Land-use change can occur across three, as well as two, dimensions. Witness the decline in the mid-twentieth century of residential accommodation above shops in high streets constructed in the late nineteenth and early twentieth centuries and its replacement by storage or offices. By the early twenty-first century, this trend had been reversed for new construction in numerous cities across the developed world as planning policies and market trends restored residential (and office) uses above shops.

How rapidly then do land uses change? Major changes in the economies of cities may work in long cycles of 50–100 years, or more, but much of office technology and retailing formats changes at a much faster rate, say 20–30 years. Changes in leisure pursuits occur within similar time periods. Not only do these elements of the urban economy change at this rate but so also do components of public policy. Ideas about the economic size and distribution of schools, primary and secondary health care, attitudes to provision for public transport and the motor car have all been subject to change over a few decades, a matter that will be considered in more detail in later chapters.

Implications for planning

There are some important lessons for planning here. Some observations that may, at first sight, appear very simple may, nevertheless, be shown to have profound implications. As built structures can be expected to last 60 years, and possibly remain in perpetuity, decisions on planning permission for individual buildings will have effects over a very long time period. Such decisions are sometimes seen as day-to-day matters affecting the *now* as opposed to development plan issues that are characterised as *forward* planning. However, all planning should necessarily be seen as *forward* by definition. Decisions on buildings are definitely long-term matters. On the other hand, development plans can be conceived as programmes for decision making, that is, they identify the decisions on development that need to be taken within the plan period. More commonly, though, a development plan conceives of the future state of an area at the end of the plan period, setting out how activities and physical form would fit together. Many would argue that it could hardly do otherwise.

The main point is, therefore, that physical form lasts a very long time, longer than the activities on it and within the buildings on it. Planning decisions need to take account of the ability of development to deal with changes over this long time period. It is often said that (and, indeed, has sometimes been said directly to the author by planning professionals) that 'you don't know what is going to happen'. The principal response to such a comment is that if this were literally true than planning would have no meaning and would be impossible to carry out. The real purpose of all planning (and not just town and country planning) is to deal with uncertainty by creating strategies that can provide for contingencies. However, somewhat ironically, the implication of the points made in this chapter is that, by and large, we do know what is going to happen. Most structures now extant will still be around in the future, as will nearly all of the new ones currently being granted permission. This will be the case despite changes in the particular activities associated with them and in society at large. Whether this situation is seen as desirable or not, the overall physical structure of urban areas will be with us for at least 60 years, and possibly indefinitely, and their design will be determined by decisions being made now. The planning decisions made now may influence future economic, demographic, social and cultural changes but they cannot determine them in the way that they determine physical form. For example, decisions on the quantity of office space are in reality more matters for *now*, or at most the medium term, whereas the decisions on the construction of office buildings are long-term ones.

Form as a constraint on activities

The next important point to be made is that, whereas urban form cannot positively determine human behaviour, it can make it either easy or difficult for people to carry out specific activities. In extreme circumstances, although a person's physical surroundings cannot compel them to carry out a particular activity, such as playing in the park, travelling by train or driving a car, it can totally prevent them from doing so. If there is no park, railway or road then there are no facilities to be used and the activities cannot take place. Even when they do exist, barriers to movement can prevent people from accessing them. It is much easier to prevent than promote.

If, as we have noted, urban form is long lasting, and also expensive to change, its ability to help or hinder human activities is of central importance. When designing an urban area, the most important question should not be the nature of the buildings or facilities that people are currently demanding, nor whether or not changing public behaviour in a desired direction might be possible in the short term. Rather it should be a question, looking at the very long term, of what range of behaviours the urban form could easily facilitate and what range of behaviours that it should make difficult. Most importantly, it is the activities that are ruled out in the long term that need to be considered when framing the policies for today.

Numerous examples of this are available from the second half of the twentieth century, particularly the 1960s and 1970s. This historic period is always worthy of study because of the dramatic rebuilding and expansion of cities in Europe and North America during this period and the changes in public attitudes and policy that followed from it. A notable one is *designing out crime*. One does not need to go down the road of 'better cities making better people', criticised by Broady (1966) as 'architectural determinism'. The *defensible space* argument of Oscar Newman (1972), the design principles of *Responsive Environments* (Bentley et al., 1985) and, subsequently, nearly all urban design texts from the mid-1980s onwards have embodied the idea that well-populated spaces with good surveillance, both within them and from adjacent buildings, permit the populace, to a large extent, to police themselves. On the other hand, spaces where people cannot be seen make it easy for criminals. In other words, the urban form does not control the propensity for criminality within the population but, rather, it provides a setting which, through its physical design, makes such activity either easier or more difficult.

Choice of mode of transport is another familiar example. The design of urban areas cannot, in itself, make a person drive a car, or use a bus or train, when they are free to do so. It can, however, make it very easy to use a car by providing parking space and appropriately designed roads, as is common, for example, in the North American outer suburb. It can also make it easy to run buses and trains efficiently by connecting development directly along rights of way for public transport. On the other hand, it can make it difficult to access areas by car by pedestrianising space and restricting car parking (or having no roads at all, as in the old city of Venice). It can also make it difficult to run buses profitably by creating extended cul-de-sac layouts and circuitous routes by road from place to place. The latter is a particularly pertinent example as it is something that is very difficult to change later, unlike pedestrianisation or provision of car parks.

A less well-trodden example is the disappearance of large backyards from new suburban houses in Australia from the 1990s onwards (Hall, 2010). There are important arguments for the provision of private open space around dwellings related to role of vegetation in drainage, microclimate, biodiversity and the energy use of dwellings as well as the more obvious ones of amenity and recreation. However, whatever position is taken on these issues, it is something that cannot now be changed without totally rebuilding all the post-1990s houses. Whatever the pros and cons, real or perceived, the change is effectively permanent and other options are ruled out. If you have a private garden, you do not have to use it. However, if you have no space for one, then there is no option.

All this would not be a problem if the physical form of urban areas was very easy to change or was in a constant state of flux of its own accord. However, as we have noted, its structure persists over very long time periods because it is difficult and expensive to change. The consequence is that it is what is ruled out that needs to be considered in the physical design of cities. If there is evidence at a certain point in time that a certain pattern of behaviour is desirable then the argument should not be about whether people could change in the short term. It should be about whether it would be facilitated in the long term and that the answer to this question should determine the design of future urban form. In other words, the design principle should be that the potential for the desirable behaviour must not be precluded in the long term.

Implications for residential density

In responding to the persistence of urban form generally, and the fact that different elements of form change at different rates, it is important to consider in more detail the matter of residential density. It is also important from a prescriptive policy standpoint, as planning policies often seek to restrict or promote changes in residential density, both up and down. We must note immediately that, in the final analysis, residential density is a matter of the number of people, as opposed to buildings or bed-spaces, per unit area. Some persons, such as tourists and family visitors, may be residing for a very short period. *Permanent* residents will be around for longer periods from a few years (much shorter than a plan period) to many decades (much longer than a plan period). They all need a place to stay and so, quite obviously, the density of people interacts with the buildings. The buildings are around for much longer periods and facilitate and regulate the density of habitation. Buildings that are *robust* in design can accommodate changes quickly and with minimum expense. Those that are not may be expensive to modify. If dwellings can be extended and subdivided into smaller apartments, and if the extensions can demolished and divisions removed relatively easily, then this will provide flexibility in the long term.

With regard to density beyond the footprint of an individual building, that is, the number of dwellings in a block or over a much wider area incorporating other uses (the *gross density*), it is much easier and cheaper to increase density than to reduce it, in response to changing circumstances. Additional dwellings may be inserted into rear gardens. Houses and gardens may be redeveloped and replaced by blocks of flats. However, once blocks of flats have been constructed their demolition and replacement can be a difficult and expensive business. To observe that all this happens is not to suggest that it is desirable but just that it occurs. If the undesirable aspects of this process are to be avoided than it would be better if the physical structure allowed for the possibility of an increase in the population density in the medium term and even a reduction again in the long term. This is not to say that this would necessarily happen, just that the possibility is allowed for.

Reference to some past historic trends as examples may make these points clearer. In many cities in Western Europe and North America developments of large single family houses were built during the latter part of the nineteenth century aimed at an expanding market amongst the upper and middle classes. Speculators overbuilt and the houses were taken over by lower-income households in multi-occupation. As the cities expanded, these former outer suburbs became part of the inner city. By the late twentieth century, these areas were subject to gentrification and underwent a reversion to high-income, single family occupation. What should be noted is the long timescales involved, in comparison with those normally associated with public policy remits, and that the buildings and streets remain the same for even longer, not just over the 100-year period but probably indefinitely. Another example involving change to the urban fabric is the housing built for lower-income groups in industrial cities throughout the nineteenth century. During the 1960s (actually late 1950s to early 1970s) many areas were completely demolished and replaced with new high-rise public housing at great expense and with a complete redrawing of the urban fabric. Although the buildings themselves were at a very high density, in terms of inhabitants per unit area of their footprints, the space left between them often meant that density over the whole area was less than that of the original terrace housing. The high-rise blocks were later found to be grossly unsatisfactory, both structurally and socially, and were demolished during the decades that followed. In many cases, they were replaced by new streets containing terraced houses and gardens although not at the same density as the nineteenth century originals. Again, the timescales and expense should be noted. However, another point that is often overlooked is that only a very small proportion of the area of the city as a whole was reconstructed in this manner. The overall structure of the city was unchanged by it. On the other hand, many Eastern European cities saw the building of a substantial amount of high-rise public housing in this period, not as local renewal but as outward extensions of the city. Such extensions were often built on a large scale, a phenomenon to be seen on an even larger scale in Chinese cities at the time of writing. This raises important questions about how long such urban form will last and the expense of making any changes to it in the long term.

The moral of these examples for the argument of this book is that it is the provision of robust building design and an urban plan (i.e. the pattern of streets and open spaces) that can create flexibility in coping with change in population density over time. In other words, density in persons per unit area is variable and difficult to determine through the planning process. The number of dwellings per unit area is longer lasting and the physical structures containing dwellings even more so. The planning process affects the physical structure. Buildings and their layout must be designed with such change in view. They must be robust in design.

References

Bentley, Ian, Alcock, Alan, Murrain, Paul, McGlynn, Susan and Smith, Graham (1985) *Responsive Environments: A Manual for Designers*, London: Architectural Press.

Broady, Maurice (1966) Social Theory in Architectural Design, *Arena: The Architectural Association Journal*, 81, pp. 149–154.

Conzen, M. R. G. (1960) *Alnwick, Northumberland, a Study in Town-Plan Analysis*, Institute of British Geographers Publication No. 27, London, George Philip

& Son. Reprinted in J. W. R. Whitehand (ed.) (1981) *The Urban Landscape: Historical Development and Management. Papers by M. R. G. Conzen.* Institute of British Geographers Special Publication No. 13. London: Academic Press.

Conzen, M. R. G. (1988) Morphogenesis, Morphogenetic Regions, and Secular Human Agency in the Historic Townscape, as Exemplified by Ludlow, in *Urban Historical Geography*, edited by D. Denecke and G. Shaw, Cambridge: Cambridge University Press, pp. 253–272.

Hall, Tony (2010) *The Life and Death of the Australian Backyard*, Melbourne: CSIRO Publishing.

Newman, Oscar (1972) *Defensible Space*, New York: Macmillan.

2 What shall we do with the private motor vehicle?

The impact of the private motor vehicle

From the mid-twentieth century onwards, there is one determinant of urban form that has had an impact like no other. The issue of designing cities for the use of the private motor vehicle is central to the question of the long-term robustness of urban form. It has always been a controversial one and it is an issue that requires a lot of clear thought.

It must be recognised that the private motor vehicle offers unparalleled convenience to the user. As long as the user also has access to fuel, roads and parking space at each end of the journey, the trip can be made at any time and at a moment's notice. The range of possible destinations is immense. As supplementary benefits, the user is insulated from the weather, has access to personal musical entertainment and can easily carry parcels, extra clothing and other large items. Apart from taxis, which are discussed below, public transport cannot, by its nature, replicate this. It is arguable that it has the potential to greatly expand possibilities and richness in life, as do all travel opportunities. (Whether or not these opportunities are taken advantage of is another matter.)

Possession of a private motor vehicle greatly increases the frequency of trips made by a person in any given time period. This, in turn, increases the demands made on energy supplies. At the time of writing, the increase in trip making is accentuated by the actual, and certainly the perceived, low cost of usage compared to other modes of transport. Whatever the actual cost of fuel, in any society and at any point in time, it will be less than the fixed costs of tax, insurance and vehicle maintenance. However painful at the time, such costs are rarely taken into account when deciding whether or not to make a particular journey and, if so, by what mode. It is the smaller, marginal, cost of fuel that may come to mind but, even here, an accurate estimate at the time of the trip would seem very unlikely. However, even if the cost of travel by private car were high, and perceived as such, it would seem unlikely that its use would cease to be popular on the grounds of the convenience it provides. The evidence for this comes from the use of taxis in urban areas. They are a very popular mode of transport in all the cities of the world even though they are the most expensive mode of transport at the point of use. Why do people pay the high fares involved when far cheaper public transport facilities are available? Clearly, people consider the comfort and convenience worth paying for if they can afford it. In terms of the arguments presented here, taxis should best be seen as equivalent to private rather than public modes of transport.

Use of the private motor vehicle also has important downsides. At the time of writing, much of the controversy surrounding the use of the private motor vehicle relates to the fuel it consumes and the pollutants produced by the burning of this fuel. The pollutants include both those directly injurious to human health and the carbon emissions that lead to global warming and climate change. Regarding the consumption of the fuel, there is the problem of reliance on a fossil fuel for which the long-term supply is finite and for which there is competing demand from the chemical industry. There is also the general extravagance in the use of energy arising from the low occupancy rate, between one and two persons per vehicle on average, coupled with the large number of trips generated. This is in contrast to public transport where vehicular occupancy will be many times higher, and fewer trips will be made per person, but which will have a lower level of perceived convenience. Another issue for urban form is the competition between the private motor vehicle and walking and cycling at very short distances, say less than 1.5 km. For short trips, there are clear arguments against frequent car use on health and energy saving grounds. As an alternative, walking and cycling are low energy, energy efficient and bring health benefits to participants. It could be argued that they are essential activities to maintain personal health.

Leaving aside the issue of the total quantity of energy used, whatever the source, the first point to note is that the issues of reliance on fossil fuels and the emission of pollutants are potentially solvable in the very long term, the time period that, it is argued here, matters for urban planning. It is technically possible to power private motor vehicles by electricity which, within the vehicle, produces little in the way of pollutants and no carbon emissions. (Whether or not the energy will be available in sufficient quantities is another question.) However, the reason for making such a bland statement here is not to present an optimistic, or even simplistic, argument for car use, rather it is to throw into relief the real problems that private motor vehicles present for the design of cities. Even if all the energy and pollutant problems were solved, the difficulties posed by the private motor vehicle would still be almost insuperable. Why this should be so will now be explained.

The spatial problem

The real problem presented by private motor vehicles is the space they take up, particularly in two dimensions. The footprint of a standard car in Europe can range from 4.2 m × 1.7 m to 5 m × 2 m with an average occupancy of 1.55 persons per vehicle. A stationary vehicle will require a significant space around it to enable it to be parked. The parking spaces alone can range from 4.8 m × 2.4 m in parts of Europe to 6.5 m × 2.5 m, or more, in North America and Australasia, with a substantial additional area of land required to enable them to be manoeuvred into this space. When moving, vehicles require much more space around them. As they travel faster, they require even more space for reasons of safety. Maximum traffic flow per vehicle lane is achieved at slightly less than 50 kph. Above this speed, the number of vehicles per hour drops because of the way the separation between the vehicles increases. The geometric design of highways for high vehicle speeds requires space for several lanes of traffic, gentle curvature and elaborate intersections, all of which are hungry for land.

Even where vehicles are restricted to very low speeds, or are stationary, and, consequently, take up less room, they still pose problems for urban design. As with many of the other issues discussed in this book, the cause of the problem appears simple and obvious when stated. For all normal activities, it is difficult for participants to carry them out while remaining in the car. The American drive-in movie is untypical. American drive-in banks and fast-food outlets cope with a passing trade but are still quite land hungry. However, for a normal cinema, department store, restaurant and gymnasium not only must cars be parked elsewhere but there will not be space in the street in front for all the customers. The proportion of land area taken up by the parking requirement will exceed that for the activities by a wide margin. This will also be the case for office blocks; the higher the block the more significant the problem. This is made visible by the size of the surface car parks at outer-suburban shopping centres in North America and Australasia. If parking is stacked up in multi-storey structures, not only is significantly greater expense incurred to support the weight of the vehicles, the building still has a very substantial footprint, not to mention an un-aesthetic bulk. The result is that the land uses have to be a considerable distance apart if the parking requirement is to be met.

Aside, though, from the social consequences, the ultimate disadvantage of the private motor vehicle is the inability to fit it in spatially. A term that was used in the US in the 1950s and 1960s was *full motorisation*. It signified a situation where everyone who was legally entitled to drive would have access to a private motor vehicle and could drive it unimpeded to any destination they chose. Attempts by individuals to do this within whatever road network was available at the time resulted in what was called, and is still called, *congestion*. The number of vehicles taking up space on each road reduced the traffic speeds, often to a very low level. From the motorist's point of view this was a problem. Road space needed to be increased to meet the demand for higher speeds. At the same time, parking needed to be provided at each end of every desired journey. In response, roads and car parks were built and continue to be built. In rural and low-density areas, and even in some urban areas off-peak, high driving speeds can certainly be obtained. However, no city has eliminated congestion, especially at peak times. Even the American examples of Los Angeles, Dallas and Houston, which have gone further than most other cities in making provision for the motor vehicle, still suffer from extensive peak period congestion, if not also at other times of the day. The reason is the impossibility of fitting in a vehicle for everyone.

This was spelled out in great detail by a now classic report from Britain in 1963, *Traffic in Towns*, often referred to as the Buchanan Report (Buchanan et al., 1963). The leader of the team that wrote it, Colin Buchanan, sincerely believed in the need for the protection of the environment from the adverse impacts of the motor vehicle. However, he also had an equally sincere belief in the inevitability of car use and of the need to accommodate this. His team carried out detailed design exercises for a selection of urban environments in England trying to resolve these opposing goals.

This required the separation of land between that required for unimpeded, that is, high speed, motor traffic but with low environmental quality, and that where environmental quality would take precedence over motor vehicle access. The *environmental areas* would be connected by a hierarchy of road types consisting of primary, secondary and local distributors and access roads.

The studies showed that the more money was spent, the closer it was possible to move towards a reconciliation between the goals. However, they also made clear the impossibility of ultimately achieving it, although the authors did realise this at the time. The designs in the report made very clear the implications for full motorisation in urban areas. In the design exercise for a small section of central London, achieving full motorisation while, at the same time, retaining a minimum degree of environmental quality did not prove possible by any possible design and the authors had to settle for a somewhat lower level of vehicle use. However, even at this lower level, reconstruction in three dimensions covered most of the land area and little of the original built form remained. The existing main roads were to be become full motorways, with grade-separated junctions, and nearly everything between them was to be rebuilt as multi-level *traffic architecture*. Political and economic reality could not even approach this. Over the following 15 years, attempts to build just the beginnings of a skeletal urban motorway network in central London were abandoned because of the expense and intense local opposition. What the Buchanan Report had demonstrated, contrary to the intentions of its authors, was the physical impossibility of accommodating anything anywhere near full motorisation within cities and the financial and political impossibility of achieving even a modest level.

This, then, is the fundamental problem. The private vehicle is land hungry. The space for roads, car parks and garages uses up a considerable area of land. Not only this, but motorways are lined by land that has little use other than to provide an environmental buffer. Such areas proliferate at intersections where the fragmented and isolated pieces of land can have no function in themselves. More than this, the width of the land used for all movement and parking increases the separation between other land uses. Severance also increases with vehicle speed. High vehicle speeds can only be maintained safely if pedestrians are kept at a distance. This results in diversions and longer journey times and distance for both pedestrians and cyclists. Attempts to reduce the impact of motor vehicles through the use of circuitous routing and cul-de-sacs increases severance, and therefore walking times, and makes it very difficult to make deliveries to dwellings and to serve them by buses. It also makes it difficult for people to find their way.

The spatial separation and severance ultimately creates an environment in which the private motor vehicle is the only practical means of getting around and use of other modes of transport, walking, cycling and buses, becomes very difficult, if not impossible. This builds in a negative factor whereby modes of travel other than the car are not easily facilitated. This has social effects. As they are not walking, people do not encounter each other on the street, so reducing sociability and security in public places. People without access to a car cannot easily make direct personal contact with others. Most interpersonal meetings, even for car drivers, are by appointment rather than casual. Shopping, education and other community activities take place within large-scale facilities that are a considerable distance apart and, therefore, can be a considerable distance from users' homes. Whereas internal spaces within shopping centres may be climate controlled and security patrolled, this does not apply to the parking areas around them. In addition to social separation, there are aesthetic problems. Roads and car parks are not attractive spaces at the best of times.

The impossibility of achieving full motorisation leaves another question. If a high level of car usage, measured against the potential demand, cannot be accommodated within urban areas, then what level should be planned for? The political reality has generally been that this was a difficult point to put directly to the public. The actual level became the maximum that could be forced into the road network that was available at a particular point in time. In other words, the level was consequential and not a matter of planning and policy. From the 1970s onwards, the hope was kept alive that a few more road schemes might do the trick in removing congestion in particular localities. In effect, this is a non-plan situation. A planned city would need an explicit understanding of the quantity and speed of road traffic that could be accommodated. Where efforts have been made at accommodating the private motor vehicle as the dominant mode of travel, it results, in practice, in a large part of the area of the city being based entirely around car use. Unfortunately, such an area can only ever serve a proportion of its inhabitants. Those that it cannot serve are disadvantaged by the spatial separation of activities consequent upon design for the car, especially where high motor vehicle speeds are facilitated. Those that are most disadvantaged may come from defined categories within society, particularly the very young and the very old.

Resolution through speed reduction

How then can urban form be designed to allow for access by private vehicles without these disadvantages? One way of attempting a solution might be to reduce the size of the footprint of the vehicle. Ever since the motor vehicle was invented, smaller designs have been introduced from time to time. Some proved more popular than others but they never became universal. To achieve a general reduction in size would require legislation and would be politically problematic. Even if it were achieved, the area of footprint of the vehicle would still be several times that of the footprint of the driver.

Where the design of urban form can produce, and enjoy, a partial solution to the accommodation of the car is in the restriction of the speed of the vehicle. As vehicles travel faster they take up more space because of the increased margin of safety required around them. Maximum throughput per vehicle lane is achieved at just under 50 kph. Above this figure, the relationship between vehicles per hour and speed becomes an inverse one. Restricting vehicles to low speeds around, or below, 50 kph will, therefore, ensure that they take up less space. Speed limits imposed by laws and signs alone can be difficult to enforce but roads can be designed such that it is near to impossible for motor vehicles to exceed a specific speed. The situation becomes self-enforcing. This approach was developed, and implemented, in Germany and the Netherlands during the 1980s and became known, from the literal translation of its German name, as *traffic calming*. It then spread from these countries to other parts of Northwest Europe during the 1990s and thence to the rest of Europe and other parts of the world. Design solutions were developed for very low speeds, almost walking pace (originally the Dutch *Woonerf*), *30 kph zones* (where large areas could be covered more cheaply but with a comparatively higher traffic speed) and the calming of main roads and shopping streets. The lower traffic speeds increased safety and reduced pollution. However, the use of, say, speed humps alone to achieve solely these ends did not represent the true value of traffic calming. What was also important was the release of road space for uses other than vehicular movement. This space could be for the benefit of the motorist through provision of additional parking but, more commonly, it was used for the benefit of cyclists and pedestrians. The distinguishing feature was an overall environmental enhancement through the employment of quality paving and planting. The beginning of the twenty-first century in Northwest Europe saw these ideas being taken much further with the removal of signs and traffic signals and the wider use of surfaces shared by all road users (motor vehicles, cyclists and pedestrians) without restriction. This approach had a particular impact when deployed in shopping streets and at urban traffic intersections.

An important consequence of the use of traffic-calming techniques in the design of new development, for both residential and retail uses, was to enable buildings to be brought closer together to enclose urban spaces. This permitted the creation of a townscape that was both sociable and aesthetic while still maintaining access for the private motor vehicle. This appears to rescue us from the initial dilemma posed by the space taken up by the motor vehicle and leads us to a more optimistic prescription for a robust urban form.

References

Buchanan, Colin et al. (1963) *Traffic in Towns: A Study of the Long-term Problems of Traffic in Urban Areas*, Reports of the Steering and Working Groups appointed by the Minister for Transport, London: HMSO.

3 Cities have not been designed for expansion

The inevitability of expansion

When taking a worldwide perspective over a long time period, one remarkable and persistent phenomenon is the continuous expansion of urban areas in the industrial and post-industrial economies. This appears to apply historically to both planned and unplanned settlements. Where there is an increase in population resulting from an increase in birth rate or from immigration then, clearly, urban expansion will follow. However, the demand for new dwellings also occurs in areas of the developed world where the population size may be stable or falling. This is because a longer lifespan, increased divorce rates and a general disinclination to share dwellings all contribute to increasing household formation.

It is true that there have, over past centuries, been cases in some parts of the world where the economy supporting a town has collapsed, especially in mining areas, and the town has contracted or even been abandoned. However, these are untypical of the general trend over both space and time. There is also the phenomenon of the decline of the centres of many, but not all, American cities. As the middle and upper income groups move to new outer suburbs the older inner suburbs become the preserve of lower-income groups with the centre used only for business activities. Eventually the business activities also move to the new *edge city* leaving large areas of the former central city effectively abandoned with little economic activity. However, this is not a planned but an unplanned phenomenon. The wider urban area around such cities is still expanding. It is confined to the US and, even there, there are notable exceptions. It does not happen in Canada and Australia, which, in common with the US, also have low-density, car-borne suburbs at some considerable distance from city centres. Whatever the causes and possible remedies, this phenomenon does not, in itself, invalidate the general observation of urban expansion.

In areas such as Northwest Europe and the north-eastern US, it is the large agglomeration of major cities interacting with each other, and with smaller settlements over a wider region, that exhibits the overall continuous enlargement. Both the city region itself and the towns within it experience urban growth. Individual towns and cities may have their growth contained by topographical features or planning policies but this may just mean that the demand will be transferred to neighbouring settlements or other parts of the city region.

To many, this continuous expansion of urban areas may appear a commonplace observation. However, its significance is not necessarily recognised in planning policy. Yes, planning policies deal with the rebuilding of urban areas and with specified new developments, even new towns, but the idea that nearly all settlements will grow continuously is not expressed in their design. If all urban areas were entirely rebuilt every 20–30 years as a matter of course then physical planning would be merely a matter of urban design carried out at the point of change. Given that this does not happen, the business of how cities can be pre-designed to cope with change should be a basic planning principle. What is remarkable is how little comment its absence causes. It is almost as if each expansion is seen as the last and it is not designed to accommodate further outward growth.

What must be stressed at this point is that it is not being suggested that there is necessarily a grand *natural law* at work or that belief in an inevitable process of economic or demographic expansion is required. It is merely a pragmatic observation that needs to be taken into account in framing public policy. What cannot be assumed is that growth will never take place at any future date. The question is then, is it wise to rest the design of the physical form of a particular urban area on the assumption that it will never expand at any future date either in area or in intensity of development? Would it not be better to adopt a precautionary principle that would allow scope for expansion even if it never happened? Recognition of the possibility of continuous growth leads to an important planning principle, to a policy of urban robustness. It is not just a matter for periphery of settlements, as the discussion below will make clear, but for all the existing urban fabric.

The problem of retrofitting the existing city

The most common way of accommodating urban growth is to expand existing settlements around their periphery. In a non-plan context, sporadic low-density housing will be built on the urban fringe. This then becomes consolidated and infilled to represent a continuous urban extension. In more planned environments, particularly where land is in short supply, large urban extensions may be constructed either at the instigation of large developers or by planning authorities. This causes a number of problems. The issue that is common to all such extensions is that they place extra loading on the infrastructure of the existing urban area especially at its centre. (Unless an *edge city* is being constructed and the former central business district has collapsed, as, unfortunately, has occurred in some American cities. However, this is a problem, not a solution.)

While it has been noted that urban areas expand, and are partially remodelled, over time, during any given period most of the existing urban fabric is not undergoing a planned reconstruction in consequence. What happens is that the new development creates pressure for a concomitant expansion of the pre-existing infrastructure within it. Increases in land values in urban centres fuel pressure for their reconstruction. Although there is a high degree of persistence in physical form in the city overall in the long term, in the short term infrastructure and service centres are subject to localised incremental and often unplanned change. Town centres have to be rebuilt, and new roads, sewers, hospitals and public transport corridors have to be retrofitted into the existing urban fabric, something that is both difficult and expensive. The pressure on existing centres can be relieved by creating new sub-centres within the urban extension but it is, unfortunately, not uncommon for areas of single-use development to be built without substantial local centres, which will inevitably depend on the existing area for services. In any case, it does not remove the problem of the pressure on the city centre for major services and on the existing infrastructure.

The issue is how can existing urban areas be designed to cope with the change brought about by urban expansion? There are a number of possible sources of land for the provision of additional infrastructure and increased services, especially retailing, hospitals and schools, within existing urban areas. The first is large-scale reconstruction and redevelopment. The replacement of obsolete housing provision from the early and mid-nineteenth century, known generally as *slum clearance*, that took place during the mid-twentieth century in the industrialised countries provided the greatest opportunity but is unlikely ever to occur again. Later periods of mass house building did not produce housing as structurally inadequate as that in the early phases of the Industrial Revolution. Economics of renewal and cultural predisposition to conservation have resulted in a large degree of reuse and conversion. Reconstruction of low-density suburban areas through urban infill certainly represents change but is a matter of an increase in the number of dwellings which then reduces that amount of spare land available for services and infrastructure – the problem rather than the solution.

A major source of developable land for the latter part of the twentieth century and early twenty-first century has been *brownfield land* arising from the obsolescence of nineteenth-century heavy industry and its immediate infrastructure. In terms of scale of provision this certainly was a boon but necessarily a one-off advantage. It is true that industrial premises from later periods will also undergo obsolescence (oil refineries and ports come to mind) but they are unlikely to provide a solution to city growth on a general basis, as they are sporadic in occurrence and not necessarily in the right places. In particular, they are rarely in existing city centres. The same goes for hospitals and schools in need of complete replacement. They cannot be relied upon as a general and continuous source of land. The reconstruction of life-expired shopping centres in more traditional street form in North America (CNU, 2005) offers in some way a more optimistic scenario in terms of what is provided, but is, in reality, a correction of the mistakes of the past in what is in effect a non-plan environment. It is not something that could be a model for the planned city.

Another source of land supply in practice has been urban green space, often playing fields in private ownership that are no longer made use of, although there may be a variety of reasons why land laid to grass and trees may not be intensively used, even when surrounded by housing. Although it is a tempting source of money for the owner, and land supply for the planning authority, it does not necessarily follow that building on it is the most appropriate form of reuse. In addition to finding space for services and infrastructure, if a city is expanding there will be the increasing need for parks and playing fields for the additional inhabitants. There is also the issue of growing food locally not just in terms of the allotments common in Britain but of urban farms, a topic that will be returned to later in this book. Planning is just as much a matter of creating new green areas as new built ones. The reason why existing green areas may be underused can be more a matter of ownership than need.

In the absence of a land supply within the existing city, there are two negative consequences that commonly arise from the retrofitting of infrastructure. One is the great expense and disruption involved in the rebuilding process. The other is that the physical and cost constraints imposed by their context often result in poorly designed facilities with a negative impact on their surroundings. This can be most noticeable with the building of motorways through existing areas. One example from the city of Taipei is illustrated by Figure 3.1. The dramatic intrusion of the retrofitted infrastructure is only too obvious. Unfortunately, it is all too common in many cities throughout the world.

Figure 3.1 The difficulty of retrofitting infrastructure with the existing urban form. A motorway in the centre of the city of Taipei

Source: Photo © Tony Hall

Issues with the design of urban extensions

The long-term solution is that, as cities expand, land should be set aside for contingencies, especially the later expansion of services and infrastructure. This may seem a simple idea. Why does it not happen? In practice, for nearly all cities around the world, urban extensions are built out as continuous built-up areas with no space left for contingencies either within them or between them and the existing city. No allowance is then possible for the growth of facilities, dwelling numbers or infrastructure in the existing areas other than by demolition and rebuilding, possibly at higher density. Schools that were once on the edge of town, with playing fields adjoining open countryside, are then surrounded by houses with no room for expansion. There can also be a lessening of the perceived identity of the new and older areas, as physical distinction is lost.

It is often the case that each extension of the urban area is seen at the time it is approved as the 'last one'. They are certainly laid out as if this was the case. A perimeter road may be constructed and a strong barrier delineating town from countryside is established. When the urban area is eventually extended, this road, with houses lining it, forms a barrier preventing new connecting road links from being built, as shown diagrammatically by Figure 3.2. Over time, as new extensions are designed on the same basis, this creates, in effect, a succession of circumferential *onion rings*. This paucity

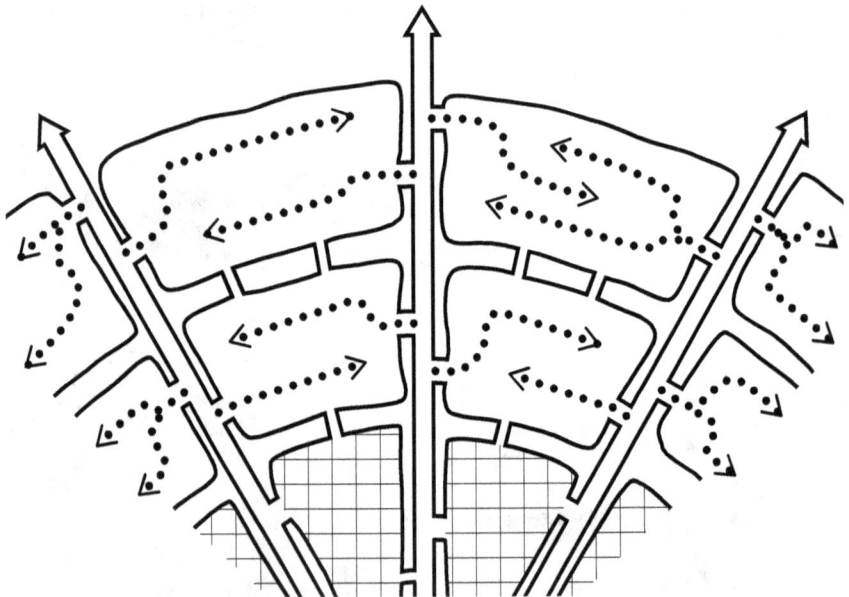

Figure 3.2 The expansion of cities by discontinuous extensions creating 'onion rings'. Without new radial roads, journey length increases and bus services become less efficient

Source: Drawn by Matthew Ryan under the direction of the author. © Tony Hall

of direct link roads is a particular problem for providing direct bus services between the new extension and the rest of the urban area. The geometry alone requires the ends of bus routes to fan out with services becoming less dense. Furthermore, this is the part of the town or city where housing will also be less dense and furthest from central facilities. As the radial distance from the centre increases, so the proportion of the area of the ring that is distant from the radial roads increases. The position of bus services is generally undermined by other aspects of the expansion of the town or city in this manner. In summary, all the circumstances give encouragement to the use of the private car and discourage the use of public transport. An example from practice is shown by Figure 3.3. The example is chosen because of the

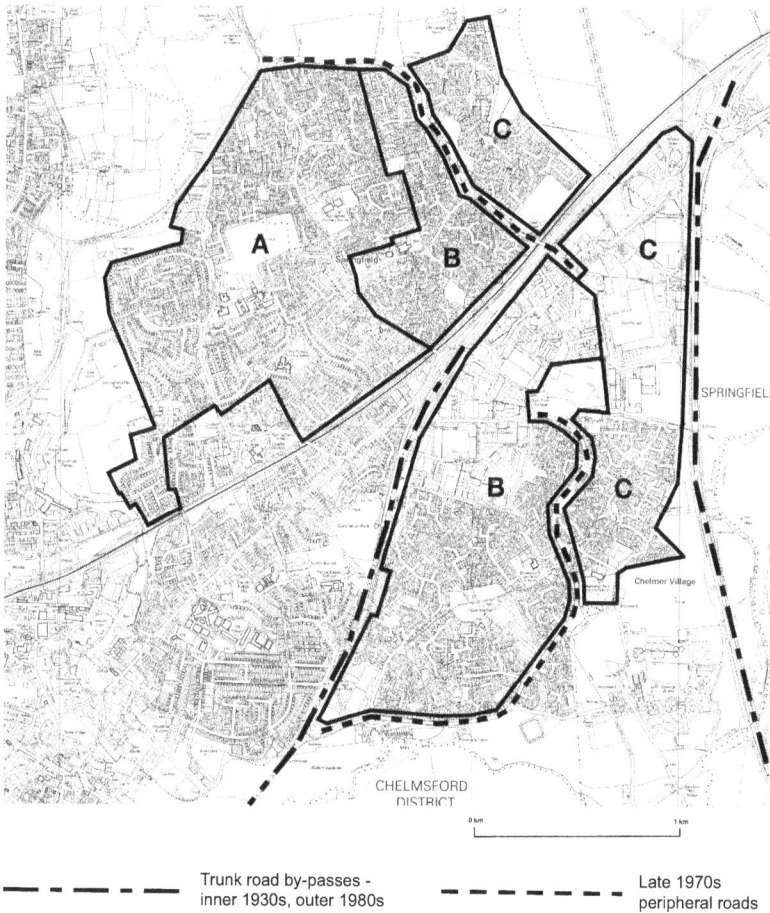

Trunk road by-passes - inner 1930s, outer 1980s   Late 1970s peripheral roads

Figure 3.3 Discontinuous expansion to the north-east of Chelmsford, Essex, UK. New perimeter roads were constructed at each stage but were later overtaken by further extensions. A: 1960s and early 1970s; B: late 1970s and early 1980s; C: late 1990s.

author's familiarity with it, not because it is unusually bad. Many others could have been used. What we see is the city expanding up to an existing bypass on some occasions and, on others, a new perimeter road being built to create a defined urban edge. Each stage of the city expansion was planned but no expansion beyond that particular stage was envisaged, and allowed for, at the time of its design.

Another issue with the design of urban extensions is that of achieving continuity of form and style, with an eye to maintaining the character of the town or city as a whole. We are not talking here about complete uniformity but the idea of maintaining the character and personality of the city as it expands over time though architectural reference points (Hall, 1996). Welwyn Garden City in England provides a rare example and shows how it could be done. Not only was the new town designed by Louis de Soissons in the 1920s with a uniform stylistic code, building materials and planting but elements of this approach were later maintained in subsequent extensions to the Garden City even if the original high aesthetic standards or attention to detail were not maintained. This can be even more important for the expansion of a village or other small-scale settlement because of the difference in the respective size of the original and the additional built form.

The rounding-off of settlements

A similar problem of the expansion of the planned city can lie in the practice of rounding-off and infilling spaces to create the two-dimensional shape of a disc. This is not something that is usually found in a non-plan settlement or, at least, not at its extremities. By non-plan settlement we mean one in which the supply of land for development is not restricted by public policy. Small settlements tend to be linear in form and larger ones are formed from a coalescing of these linear structures. Settlements expand along lines of communication. In the history of the pre-industrial city these were roads and waterways. Industrialisation brought railways and tramways and in the twentieth century roads for motor vehicles. This comes about because of the way people move along these routes in the course of their daily business. Land values are highest along these principal routes. Over time side lanes penetrate into their hinterland, where values are lower. This pattern of movement remains the same in the planned city even when it has acquired the disc shaped form.

The way that movement is shaped by the connectivity of streets has been amply demonstrated by the *space syntax* of Bill Hillier (1984). His work shows how high connectivity is linear in form along main roads and also how areas with low connectivity can exist close to, but behind, through routes. Kevin Lynch's classic work on mental maps (Lynch, 1960) also showed the significance of paths and their intersections for finding the way. Although his formalism included districts, the way that people found their way to them was plain to see. For more anecdotal and personal evidence, the author was struck while growing up in the southern suburbs of Greater London by how trips for working and shopping were normally along the main radial routes. Trips to destinations located on other radials, even when shorter, were comparatively infrequent.

There are a number of other reasons why the unplanned city is not disc shaped. Topographical features can make building in some places, such as steep hillsides and the flood plains of rivers, very expensive, if not totally impractical. Where towns have grown up around a crossing point or defensive position on a river, the flood plain of the river valley will reinforce, and prevent, the coalescing of the settlement along the radial routes.

In the planned city, development is confined by public policy to specified areas of land. This may be defined by an overall urban footprint but, whatever the procedural format, there will be areas of open countryside where development would not normally be allowed and areas designated for new building in and around existing settlements. The tendency is for development to be permitted between the radial routes before allowing further expansion of the city, thus creating the disc shaped form. Why should this be? Rather than deriving it clearly from the goals and objectives, plans often take it for granted and offering little explanation.

Where reasons are given, the one most commonly advanced is that of not fragmenting the countryside. This planning principle has certainly been central to British planning from the mid-twentieth century onwards, if not earlier. The principle holds, with much justification, that the efficiency of recreational agricultural uses and preservation of the natural ecology can best be guaranteed if there are large expanses of countryside uninterrupted by urban development. Another important principle is that settlements should not be allowed to coalesce. The reasons have rarely been made as explicit as they have with the previous principle but some will be offered later in this book. However, as significant as these two principles are they do not, in themselves, require the rounding-off of settlements. On the contrary, if free-standing settlements should not coalesce then, by the same token, why should the radial extensions of cities be allowed to?

The issues of land values and topographical constraints that, as we have noted, shape the unplanned city would also seem to apply to the planned one. Moreover, there are other strong reasons against rounding-off that will form a recurrent theme within this book. People need access to open space. Ideally, this should be accessible on foot or bicycle, especially when considering the needs of children. Playing fields, in particular, take up significant areas of land and the space between the radial roads can provide room for them. This space also allows for expansion and retrofitting of new infrastructure, especially new roads. Hilltops that have not been built on can provide visual breaks between neighbourhoods, not only providing aesthetic appeal but also reinforcing a local sense of identity. Concern about the proper management of the flooding of rivers leads to the protection of flood plains from development. Open space between settlements also allows for sustainable drainage. Smallholdings adjacent to urban areas can supply fresh fruit and vegetables with a minimum of transport.

Given the number and strength of arguments against the rounding-off of the city, the arguments in favour appear to be reduced to those of tidy-mindedness. Looking at a map in two dimensions, built-up areas with green spaces in-between them does indeed make the use of land look fragmented and, by implication, wasteful. The experience on the ground in three dimensions is, however, quite different.

Are new settlements the answer?

Is then the construction of new towns the answer? Central to the argument is the timing of provision of infrastructure. If a new town or city is designed as a whole then the quantity of infrastructure required will be clear from the beginning. Unfortunately for the provider, a large part must also be provided from the beginning. Even if phased, for the construction of the new town a lot of infrastructure will still be needed up front. There will be a need for a substantial and complete set of roads, schools, hospitals etc. from an early date. It is often argued that this is the problem for housing development in the form of new settlements as opposed to the incremental growth of existing towns. However, the argument that it is a problem implies that the same amount of infrastructure would be not be required in the expansion of existing towns and that it would be less expensive to provide it. Is this, in fact, the case?

The commonly made case is that existing urban areas already have the infrastructure and so any increase would be marginal. Closer examination, though, quickly reveals flaws in this argument. It may be the case that a particular town or city has excess capacity in some, or all, of its facilities. However, as it expands inexorably, as cities invariably do, then the increase in demand will mean that the capacity limit must eventually be reached. Over time all the facilities will fill up. This is a consequence of the persistence of urban form coupled with the inevitability of growth. A town or city will either have its infrastructure at capacity or will reach this position in the course of time. At some time in the future, therefore, the capacity of the infrastructure must be increased to meet the needs of the expanded population. The children will need additional school places, the sick will need more hospital beds and there will be a need for more and wider roads and more capacity in bus services. Although, in the first instance, marginal alterations to existing facilities will suffice, over time major extensions will be needed and eventually new free-standing construction will be required. Marginal additions to the existing infrastructure cannot be made indefinitely. At some stage the facility will have to be built or replaced with a larger version. For example, people living in an urban extension may use local shops for some needs but they will also shop in the existing centre. This will increase the demand on the existing centres bringing about pressure to expand both outwards and upwards. Costs would remain equivalent to those for a new town if space had been allowed for expansion in the layout of the existing urban area. Unfortunately, this is almost never the case. There is unlikely to be room left to expand the existing facilities. Land will need to be acquired and existing uses replaced and buildings demolished. All this will be costly and the cost may exceed those of building entirely new facilities on a greenfield site. In addition there is the disruption and dislocation caused to existing residents and businesses. Given the continuous expansion of towns and cities in the long term this disruption will not be a one-off event but an ongoing problem.

Costs can be very high. Schools can sometimes be extended fairly cheaply but hospitals cannot. Rail-based public transport can be put underground but doing the same for roads is very expensive because of the ventilation requirements. Space may become available because of the obsolescence of large-scale commercial or industrial facilities but this is unlikely to create the linear and continuous right of way required by new roads. The land may not necessarily be in the right place, of the right quantity or available at the right time. Finding space otherwise needs expensive land acquisition and demolition of existing structures. There is a temptation to find room by building on public open space. This, however, will reduce the provision of parks and playing fields just as demand for them is increasing. Rebuilding of city centres and inner-city areas will create all the problems referred to above and increase the demand for public open space in the very areas where it is expensive to provide it. Such rebuilding places pressure on the same infrastructure as will be used by the inhabitants of the additional peripheral development.

Even if a new town is constructed on a greenfield site, it will inevitably be faced, in the fullness of time, with incremental expansion. This has, for example, been the case with nearly all the British new towns. The argument leads, therefore, to the need for all towns, and extensions to towns, to be designed for expansion and for the capacity of the infrastructure to be continually increased. As was argued earlier, even if new settlements were to be constructed and planning policies for them, and selected existing towns, were to be in place to restrict their growth, it is somewhat risky to maintain that they will never, in the very long term, be subject to any expansion.

This is not an argument against new towns – on the contrary it is an argument for them. What is being said is that the new towns are likely to be more cost-effective in providing infrastructure than expanding existing urban areas, even if most of the costs are up front. What must be noted, though, is that a substantial new town will also be under pressure to expand and should be designed accordingly. However, it has the opportunity of being so designed, unlike an older urban area. This argument points in the direction of expansion by means of a combination of repeated small new settlements that would not be expanded in themselves. In other words, the pressure for expansion would be met by repeatedly building new settlements near to an existing urban area. This is going to work only if such settlements are well connected to each other such that their retail, health and educational facilities can be shared.

The issue of thresholds

This argument leads, unfortunately, to another planning dilemma. As we have said that urban form persists over a long period, how much infrastructure and other facilities should be built initially, in relation to a given population, and what allowance should be made for change over a long period? This is a difficult question because, as has also been acknowledged, the demands for, and nature of, the infrastructure can change quicker than the overall physical form. On the other hand, over-engineering to create slack in the system can be very expensive and not covered by immediate financial returns.

Underlying this problem is the issue of thresholds, the minimum number of people required to support different local facilities. Schools, hospitals, buses, trains and shops do not expand continuously with increasing demand but have specific thresholds at which they are considered viable. New settlement design should be consistent with these thresholds or, at least, ought to be in the planned city. For example, the neighbourhood unit principle, as employed in the British Mark 1 New Towns in the 1950s, incorporated the idea that local people should be able to walk to local shops and a primary school. The walking distance criterion is a laudable one that will be returned to later in this book. This assumed not only that a particular size of neighbourhood might be viable on educational grounds, providing sufficient children for the primary school, but that it would also form an economic catchment area for local shops and that this relationship would remain constant over time. Unfortunately, this has not proved to be the case. The format of shopping in response to uses of the car changed drastically during the second half of the twentieth century. The pressure to continue such changes, and take them further, remains. The size and catchment populations of not only schools but also health centres and other community facilities also changed over the same period and with them the viability of the neighbourhood principle.

It is important to pause to note that the economic and social components of the issue of viability are both subject to mediation through the political process. For example, the size of schools and the ages at which children change schools are related to educational as well as economic principles and this can be a matter of choice of values and public debate. The same is true for the size of hospitals and other health care facilities which, in turn, affects their accessibility and catchment area. Local facilities, by definition, will need to be small and in large numbers. On the other hand, as the wealth of developed countries increases, so does the real cost of labour, leading to pressure for greater efficiency in its use. Such pressure may find an outlet in larger institutions. For hospitals, there is the additional cost of special equipment and the need to make the most efficient use of it. Very large hospitals will be few and far between and the implication of this for their accessibility can be a point of concern in public policy. The trend to greater economies of scale can be countered by subsidy from the public purse. The same is true for public transport operations where viability is an issue but so is subsidy. Their efficiency can be affected by investment and technological innovation. The overall point is that the unit size and catchment area of infrastructure is subject to both economic pressures and government decision. They are not fixed and there is no implication that any particular change would be permanent. For example, a change of values in public policy could bring about a return to smaller schools and smaller, more local, hospitals. In summary, therefore, the population thresholds needed to support particular facilities are not fixed over long periods of time. Enduring patterns of settlement cannot reflect them either.

A way forward?

As we have seen, the overall physical form of settlements endures and urban areas tend to expand. Retrofitting and rebuilding is then expensive. Herein lies the dilemma for planning. What are needed are physical forms that have all their initially required infrastructure but are robust over time, that is, they need a minimum of rebuilding as infrastructure thresholds change. The continuous unbroken extension of built-up areas will not provide this. New towns offer an initial advantage but need to be designed to be extendable. What are really needed are new settlements that are linked together such that if a service is not available in one it is possible to travel cheaply and conveniently to another one where it may found. It would represent a considerable overall challenge and a comprehensive solution is unlikely to be value free. Nevertheless, it would be a step forward if the relationship between the more robust form and values in public policy were made explicit and comprehensible. How this could be achieved will be addressed in the next and subsequent chapters.

References

CNU, Congress for the New Urbanism (2005) *Malls into Main Streets*. Chicago, IL: Congress for the New Urbanism.

Lynch, Kevin (1960) *The Image of the City*, Cambridge, MA: MIT Press.

Hall, A. C. (1996) *Design Control: Towards a New Approach*. Oxford: Butterworth-Heinemann.

Hillier, Bill (1984) *The Social Logic of Space*, Cambridge: Cambridge University Press.

4   Deriving form

A goal-driven approach

In this chapter we will try to start to put the design of urban form on a systematic basis. This will require an attempt at clear thinking about how it can be derived from general goals. It will be argued that it is indeed possible to generate patterns of form by a goal-driven process. If goals can be agreed, by no means a trivial matter, patterns of urban form can be deduced from them. There is, of course, nothing new in making this attempt. The proper role of goals and objectives in planning has been recognised since at least the late 1960s, although it has not always been taken as seriously and literally as it should. It would seem eminently reasonable to state that there should be a clear rationale behind all proposals for development. However, to demonstrate that a deductive process for the logical justification of such proposals, and to show that they are the consequence of the goals, is perfectly feasible is far more ambitious. What has been characterised as a *rational model* in planning has rarely met with total espousal in practice although its outward forms and labels are applied almost universally.

One of the problems has been the lack of sound goals. Goals of the 'a good town to live in' type, although a laudable sentiment, do not lead easily and directly to design qualities and criteria for the location of development. They are often satirised as *motherhood and apple pie* statements, that is, ones that everyone can agree with. They can be criticised on at least two main counts. Firstly, they do not engage with the political decision-making process. Secondly, they do not lead directly to specific outcomes. What they can lead to, and give apparent support for, is a situation in which there are, in effect, no real goals at all.

From time to time, many people within the planning profession and academia have held, and some may still hold, that planning is predominantly a process rather than a goal-seeking and normative activity. The idea that planning should be confined to a *value free* process was particularly fashionable in some quarters during the *systems thinking* period in planning during the late 1960s. It could be characterised as akin to the role of a referee or umpire in a sports match: there to make sure that the players keep to the rules and remaining neutral with regard to the outcome. In planning, the process is seen as taking the role of an intermediary between the stakeholders, such as property developers and local residents, to ensure that equity and justice prevail. The idea of a planner acting only as a *referee* has often continued to exist as a decision-making model not because of a theoretical justification but because of a reluctance to allow intervention in the development process expressed through the political process. This was the case in Britain during the 1980s, and is to be found in many parts of North America and Australasia at the time of writing. Extensive rules and regulations in the form of voluminous zoning ordinances and development codes stand in contrast to poor outcomes in terms of the quality of urban form. The problem is that real planning involves intervention in the development process and this intervention is value-loaded. A real plan should be content, not procedure. An absence of planning creates one situation and planning intervention another, both representing a set of values. Furthermore, this intervention has widespread and long-term effects with decisions affecting people over wide areas, and the effects can last for decades if not centuries.

Another issue is that the goals are not necessarily mutually exclusive, that is, they may overlap, and neither do they necessarily fit into a tree-type hierarchy. Such hierarchies are artificial and their simplicity is seductive and misleading. To list goals as apparently parallel and independent is not only misleading but also lacking in utility. It encourages the *motherhood and apple pie* idea that implies that it may be possible to deliver all that is specified all of the time. Goals with utility interact with each other both positively and negatively, creating a complex web. Complexity is of the nature of the real world and analysis of the real world should bring this out.

Criteria are as important as goals. They have a role in planning for dealing with uncertainty: 'if A occurs then B will apply'. However, this can never be the whole story. In the absence of prescriptive goals and objectives this leads to a situation where sites for development tend to be evaluated against unspoken criteria or criteria that appear extraneously without clear links to the planned goals. It engenders a reactive attitude to planning and to policies. Rather than be the predominant type of planning control, the reactive mode should apply only to matters that are not essential concerns. What is needed are proactive principles of the type 'A is sought therefore B is required'. This comes only from goals that are clear and prescriptive and can also interact with the political decision-making process. How this can lead to physical outcomes will be pursued within this chapter.

Nomenclature

Part of the problem with the use of goals has been the use of more general words to cover a variety of intentions. The words *goal, objective* and *criterion* may have distinct dictionary meanings but they are often used to refer to different items by different authors. In addition, planning documents and books on urban design often contain other terms, such as *policy, quality, principle* and *standard*, that convey important ideas but do not have fixed definitions between countries and over long time periods. That there may be a variation in the use of these words should not be surprising. It is a testimony to the complexity of the issues and the way that theory and practice have been continually evolving.

For the purposes of this book, a set of terms with reasonably fixed meanings will be needed in order to obtain some internal clarity and consistency. As long as these meanings are established, then it should be possible for other authors and practitioners to translate them into the terms used in other contexts.

- *Goal* will be used to denote an aspiration for a value or course of action. There will be higher level goals, such as *pursuit of quality of life,* that give rise to a set of goals and the goals within these sets may then lead to sub-goals.
- *Objective* will be used to denote something to be achieved that is particular to a locality, as specified within a development plan, brief or other local policy document, for example *number of dwellings to be constructed.*
- *Criterion* will refer to a general basis for judging and guiding action, for example 'dwellings should be located within walking distance'.
- *Quality* will be used for properties that urban form should possess if they are to fulfil the goals, for example *permeability* and *legibility.*
- Underlying the qualities there will be theory, conceptual structures and technical knowledge.
- Pursuit of the *qualities* will lead to specific *types* of urban form.
- The *types* will possess derived *characteristics.*

It will be maintained that there is a deductive line of reasoning between these terms, as illustrated by Figure 4.1. However, it is the line of reasoning which is sequential, not necessarily the links between the values. The values covered by the terms set out above will have a complex pattern of interaction between all of them. They rarely form a simple hierarchy. Fortunately, it will be found that, by and large, they reinforce each other and pull together, rather than pulling apart, but this is a fortuitous, rather than a necessary, consequence.

Goals that impact on urban form

Let us now consider the goals that impact on urban form. It is not suggested that they will be an exhaustive list of all possible goals, just those that affect the physical form of settlements. From Chapter 1 we can note that:

- cities contain buildings, public and private spaces, infrastructure for transport, water and power;
- these all tend to have a very long lifespan, 50 to many hundreds of years.

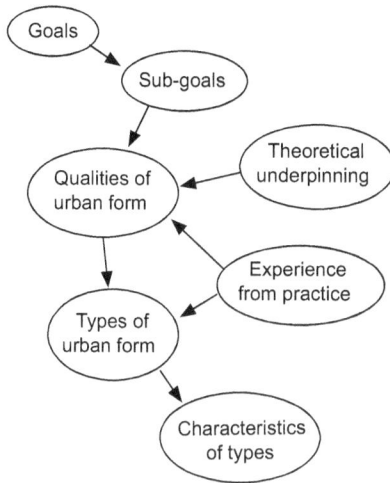

Figure 4.1 The sequential relationship between goals, qualities, types and characteristics

Source: Diagram © Tony Hall

They are there to provide:

- somewhere to live;
- recreation and enjoyment;
- services and shops;
- employment;
- health facilities;
- educational facilities.

These tend to evolve over time and their requirements may change over a shorter time span measured in decades. If we are talking, as we are, about a planned city, how can the physical form be designed to facilitate human activities over time? It will be argued that a typology of the desired form can be derived from general goals, in particular the pursuit of the quality of life, covering enjoyment, health and security, and the pursuit of sustainability. It is true that governments pursue more goals than this. Economic prosperity, supplies of food and mineral resources, all come to mind. However, they do not bear so directly on the argument of this book, with one exception. This is an economic goal that has underlain the argument of Chapter 3, that of financial prudence. This leads to a desire to minimise changes to the physical form of cities because of the expense it would entail. The need for *robustness* in the design of cities follows in consequence.

It is suggested that two broad, overarching goals, the pursuit of *quality of life* and of *a sustainable environment,* can form the basis for the planning of a robust urban form. They are powerful generators of planning sub-goals and design qualities impacting on the built environment. It has been fortunate that, from the 1990s onwards, the situation in most countries has been strengthened by the emergence of the pursuit of sustainability as a major issue and a return to favour of urban design in a new and more relevant form. These have together helped to create a new consciousness of the significance of physical form.

Pursuit of quality of life

Seeking improvement of the quality of life for the people should be the basis of all planning. In the final analysis, this can be the only justification of the constraints that the planning system places upon individual liberty. It is, of course, a more complex and substantial goal than might be imagined at first sight. The difficulty that planning practitioners have in developing the goal occurs early on in the process. How does it link through to standard planning issues and how can planning outcomes be derived from it? The way forward is to argue that goals should embody *responsiveness*: examining people's needs and attempting to respond to them. It could be taken as axiomatic that people would like to have surroundings that are beautiful or, at the very least, pleasant. However, the subjectivity surrounding this concept has long been a concern for both professionals and politicians. Issues surrounding personal taste (such as how taste may be expressed through market forces, the competition between higher and popular culture and the long-term nature of aesthetic values) have bedevilled debate and have often been used to support a retreat from planning intervention. Two points must be made. Firstly, it is because of this subjectivity that planning is placed under political control rather than seen as solely a technical exercise. A forum is thereby provided for deciding subjective matters. Secondly, the subjective element is only part of the story and closer analysis reveals much, possibly the greater part of the argument, to be objective.

A number of very important, and very practical, sub-goals stem from the *quality of life* goals. They are normally associated with the qualities underlying *urban design* as an area of practice. The italics are meant to imply that this is a convenient term in current use, much like *town planning* in which the *town* is not to be taken too literally. *Design* must be seen here as a creative decision-making process that can be as much rural as urban. The point was made above that the planning principles should be responsive to human needs. Beyond the fundamental and axiomatic need for shelter, there are a number of needs that come to the fore in the design of settlements and could be adopted as goals. People need to:

- have pleasant, ideally beautiful, surroundings;
- feel safe and secure;
- have the opportunity for privacy;
- have the opportunity for peace and quiet;
- have the opportunity to be sociable;

- be able to travel and have access;
- be able to find their way easily;
- have the opportunity for recreation and exercise.

Meeting some of these can be easier than others because of the ways in which people's personal interests interact. Some of them pull altogether and some pull in opposite directions. Some are consistent with the sustainability goals and some tend to work against them. Often, urban design tasks either assume qualities or promote them in an advocacy role. The danger here is that the claim to respond to *people's needs* may be countered on occasions by *the people* saying that they want something different. In other words, what happens when the public likes things that planners say is bad for them?

Is planning concerned with 'giving people what they want'? There are many problems with a goal such as this. Do people actually know what they want? Even if they did, could these wants be clearly expressed and articulated? If everyone could have what they wanted all of the time then not only planning but all government would be redundant. Government in general, and planning in particular, are necessary because everybody cannot have what they want all of the time, even if these wants could be precisely identified. In particular, planning cannot provide people with all they say they want as some of these desires run counter to the achievement of the sustainable and sociable city. It is inevitable that there will have to be compromises in any city and the task will be one of optimisation.

In other words, it cannot be assumed that all needs do not conflict with each other or that the people's desires are consistent. The solution is to analyse the interaction of the needs in order that a political decision can ultimately be made on a fairly rational basis. The analysis of how needs combine and conflict leads to quite specific design principles, referred to here as *qualities*. Qualities can be identified that are value-loaded but which, if adopted, can offer a way forward to optimum and practical outcomes. Historical analysis may explain why people have derived these principles for themselves over many centuries as towns grew. The sub-goals of *quality of life* can be powerful generators of these *qualities*.

For example, the need for people to have a healthy environment, free from pollution and with opportunities for recreation, lends itself to quantitative expression. Children's play, and the sporting activities of both adults and children, can be, and are, expressed quantitatively. Regarding the visual perception of the environment, the whole corpus of writing on urban design since the 1960s has attempted to systematise people's requirements. The townscape movement has gone some way to codifying the way people perceive their surroundings not only aesthetically but also with regard to the more practical question of how they find their way. Since the 1970s, urban design principles have emphasised the importance of privacy and, since the 1980s, the promotion of security and sociability through the layout of towns. These examples will be amplified within this chapter.

Pursuit of a sustainable environment

This is the more recent of planning goals, effectively coming to the fore only during the 1990s, but it is nevertheless a most powerful and significant one. Discussion of sustainability issues is widespread and ongoing. What is needed here is to make some points that will assist the task of this book. The pursuit of sustainability has two aspects:

- prudent conservation and management of resources, and
- minimisation of negative externalities, normally pollutants;

which will involve:

- minimising use or at least the avoidance of excessive use;
- reuse, recycling and replacement;
- seeking of renewable sources.

These overlap with the goal of financial prudence, as referred to above. This leads to sub-goals that apply to water, energy, land and biodiversity, generally, and to food and building materials, more particularly:

- minimisation of water use;
- minimisation of energy use;
- maximisation of biodiversity;
- prudent management of land;
- prudent management of building materials.

The minimisation of pollution will apply to:

- domestic waste;
- construction waste;
- industrial waste;
- carbon emissions.

These are all practical and quantifiable matters that can be useful in deriving desired qualities of urban form. The one that is the least straightforward, though, and needs some further clarification is the *prudent management of land*. It is often argued that new settlements should be planned so as not to waste land. They should be compact and not spread out. Land is seen as a scarce resource. On the other hand, there are arguments the other way that land is not in short supply and that urban development takes up only a very small proportion of what is available (Hall P., 2005). It is maintained that other factors should place a limit on the growth of a city, if this happens at all. To a certain extent these arguments are at cross-purposes. It is true that in looking at the whole planet, whole countries and even large regions of countries, only a small proportion of the total land area is built over. There are very large areas of the world where the terrain and climate are such as to preclude large-scale urbanisation. However, at the same time, land is very valuable in places where many people and organisations compete for it, such as in the centres of cities. What a sub-goal should express is that urban form should be designed to optimise the use of land in those locations where it is in high demand and in short supply.

Deriving qualities of urban form

Finding the way in pleasant surroundings

The sub-goals that are probably most easily appreciated by the public are *finding your way* and the *desire for pleasant or beautiful surroundings* and these lead to the quality of *legibility*, as it is technically known. Consideration of legibility must start with the classic work of Kevin Lynch on *mental maps* (Lynch, 1960). He asked lay people to draw their own maps of how they found their way through urban areas. His analysis of the mental maps led him to his well-known list of physical elements that people use for navigation: routes, nodes, landmarks, neighbourhoods and edges. The analysis responds to people's needs and behaviour. It is based on human perception. It draws attention to how people move through urban areas. The same is true of the work of the other classic figure of the *townscape* school, Gordon Cullen. In his seminal book *Townscape* (Cullen, 1961), he also analysed people's perceptions of the physical environment and their movement through it. His work drew attention to something that is fundamental to the aesthetics of the town, the idea of *enclosure*. The enjoyment and aesthetics of enjoying urban areas comes from the feeling of being enclosed in three dimensions. This can occur in different ways by different means and to different degrees but is, nevertheless, fundamental. It helps people to define spaces and relate themselves to it. Views and vistas can be important but they exist by virtue of the contrast with the more enclosed spaces. The varied sequence of spaces experienced by a person passing through an urban area is what Cullen termed *serial vision*. Many other factors affect the viewer's perception of the environment in Cullen's analysis but these are the most important. Cullen in his time was criticised from some quarters for pursuing a particular aesthetic and promoting the picturesque. To see this as a failing is largely to miss the point. In addition to the purely functional requirements for finding their way, it is right that people gain pleasure from their surroundings. The design of these surroundings therefore needs to respond to what people find pleasurable and aesthetic analysis is needed to determine its components. The components can then be developed within urban design and the planning process. People like the picturesque and it is important to respond to this desire as long as it is understood that it is not the only aesthetic quality involved. Neither is the pleasure just that of being a tourist. A feeling of well-being when going about daily work and relaxing from these tasks is important for health and efficiency.

The term *legibility* was emphasised in the influential manual *Responsive Environments* (Bentley et al., 1985) which also drew attention to further qualities, *visual appropriateness* and *richness*. *Visual appropriateness* relates to ensuring the appearance of buildings relates to their function. This is a fundamental principle in helping ordinary people not only to find their way but also to orient themselves generally in the urban environment. *Richness* refers to the need for a variety of sensory experiences to obtain enjoyment of urban surroundings. *Transparency*, by which those at street level are observed directly from the road, for example, in shops and in turn observe the street, aids the achievement of legibility and also of the pursuit of the quality *richness*.

There is another term developed in *Responsive Environments* that can also be raised at this point, *personalisation*. It can be held to be an additional sub-goal of the pursuit of *quality of life* that dwellings (and to a lesser extent small shops and offices) can be adapted to reflect the tastes of the occupier. This can be in conflict with other aesthetic objectives, but not necessarily so. Small areas of private space in front of buildings can facilitate this through planting and garden ornaments. Personalisation can also be achieved through modification of the material and shape of a building. Within the limits imposed by other objectives (especially aesthetics) this is something to be encouraged.

Over and above these considerations, there is also the more subjective one of *character* and/or *sense of place*, stemming from the goal of pursuit of quality of life. The sub-goal of *desire for beautiful surroundings* leads to:

*   conservation of heritage, deriving from long-term cultural values;
*   enhancement of existing, or creation of new, character.

Both imply that some physical characteristics of a locality will be retained and some replaced. They also require a means of defining *character* or *sense of place* and expressing this in a way that can guide the development process. It is important to note that the outcome will be the result of an interaction between the existing physical features (including topography and planting) and aesthetic goals and objectives. However, as was explained and emphasised in Chapter 1, physical features can last for substantial periods. Conservation by its very nature implies that they are being retained for a very long time. This implies the long-term maintenance of cultural values, indeed for a longer period that many economic and social trends. This returns us to an overall theme of this book – that urban form is, at one and the same time, long lasting and goal driven. The fact that this may appear superficially contradictory is the very point. Resolving such issues is why planning is necessary for the city and it is a means by which the more detailed policies are generated.

The account so far may be seen as having a somewhat deterministic ring to it as it takes insufficient account of the degree of application and of local judgement and the implementation process on a political context. In practice this would be modified by the particular objectives in a development plan relating to local circumstances. It is possible to set out objectives for a plan area that will govern its aesthetics (Hall, 1996). There may be ones that indicate the historic periods that are valued and to what degree. They may also set out the overall image desired for a city and how it is viewed from different standpoints such as its entrances and exits. There is also a need to recognise that any objective must be qualified by *degree of intervention*. It is neither practical nor desirable for planning control to be uniformly strict.

Pursuing sociability and security

The sub-goals of the pursuit of *safety*, *sociability*, *privacy* and *quietude* are more problematic because of the potential they have to be in conflict with each other. In an unconstrained situation, people will say that they want to be away from other people because of the value placed on privacy and peace and quiet. Within the public realm, at a local level, it is the role of urban design to resolve conflicts between community and privacy. Residents, and sometimes the police, will want to restrict strangers from passing along their road through the provision of cul-de-sacs, or other means. On the other hand, contact between people and surveillance of people by others, not only in public places but from buildings looking on to public spaces and from public looking at buildings, is how community safety can really be achieved. It also is the means of achieving greater sociability. If the layout of streets and public spaces encourages people to encounter each other, then a more vibrant and enjoyable community can result.

At a broader citywide scale, there is a similar potential conflict. Those who can afford it, perhaps the majority, achieve safety, quiet and privacy by separating themselves off at a very low density. They will argue that this will also protect them against crime by being remote from criminal elements in society. This is one of the main driving forces behind the very low-density suburb (another being the use of the private car) and, for those who can afford it, commuting from houses located in the countryside. This is a real choice that people make and it is popular with those who make it. It responds to their needs and this must be recognised. However, the problem is that it conflicts with the other goals. The sub-goal of sociability can only be achieved at low density by undertaking large numbers of motor vehicle trips. This is a major disincentive. It is possible to argue that there is a general trend in society, especially in the low-density suburb, to less and less sociability and that this is to be deprecated. If we bring into play the goals relating to the pursuit of sustainability, they would conflict with the promotion of large areas of low-density settlement. It is extravagant in the use of energy for transport and in the use of land and other resources.

The logic of the argument following from the need to obtain a resolution of the potential conflicts between the sub-goals leads, therefore, to a medium-to high-density settlement with high degrees of sociability, crime controlled by mutual surveillance and privacy and quietude achieved through urban design solutions. Since at least the mid-1980s, urban design thinking has provided a set of qualities that expresses this. In addition to those discussed in the previous section, there is *permeability*, originally a term developed in the work leading up to *Responsive Environments* (Bentley et al., 1985) which is now a common term although not all always properly understood. It means that the layout of settlements should be such that people can pass through them with maximum chance of meeting others, observing people in buildings, and being surveyed from them, but which at the same time responds to occupants' privacy. It does not imply a maximum number of public routes but, on the contrary, is a way of minimising them. The work of Hillier (1984) on *space syntax* also demonstrates, through mathematical reasoning, the effectiveness of a grid of streets (not necessarily rectilinear) for achieving the goal. The point is that redundant pathways and cul-de-sacs are less likely to be chosen by people when getting about and, therefore, will have fewer people on them and should be avoided.

The apparent conflict between the sub-goals can also be resolved through the traditional device of having public fronts and private backs. This results in the form of the *perimeter block* (see Figure 4.2) which also has the advantage of increasing security. This form has been traditional because it works in reconciling apparently conflicting goals. It is discussed more fully in the following chapter on the typology of desired form.

Pursuit of environmental quality

The sub-goal of the *promotion of biodiversity* has implications beyond the protection of existing habitats. It also implies the promotion of *green areas* within urban areas and even the weighing of the merits of different types of green area against each other. The provision of planted areas in towns and cities is important for maintaining a range of animal and plant species. This is reinforced by the need for *private gardens* (which also follow from privacy goals) and urban woodlands. The interconnecting area of soft landscaping created by adjoining rear gardens hosts a high degree of biodiversity. The density and variety of the planting in a domestic garden is something that is not found elsewhere. For example, farming monocultures, and even playing fields, have very limited biodiversity in comparison. (The playing fields are, of course, needed but the gardens and woods are needed also.) Authors have remarked upon the number of plant species to be found in back gardens in European cities (Pyšek, 1989; Gilbert, 1991). From studies of English gardens, Gilbert draws attention to the variety of vegetation to be found not only in planted beds but also in lawns, ponds and on walls. He also describes the variety of the associated fauna which includes insects and other small

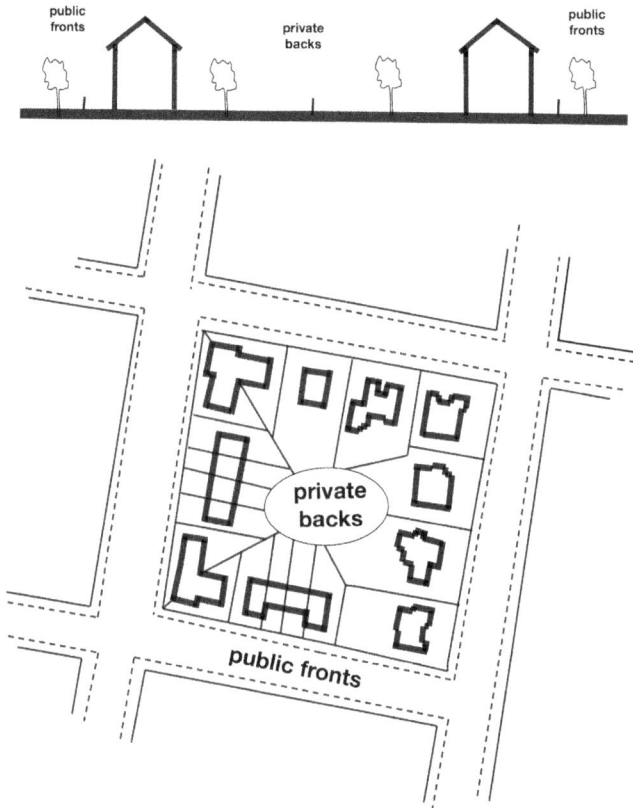

Figure 4.2 The principle of the perimeter block incorporating public fronts and private backs

Source: Diagram © Tony Hall

creatures. He makes the valuable point that all this is not dependent solely on a 'wild' garden.

The sub-goals relating to the management of water as a resource have direct implications for urban form. In many parts of the world, large-scale measures to deal with both floods and shortages are required but these lie outside the scope of this book. What concerns us here is the more general and detailed issues for the management of water within urban areas known as *sustainable drainage* (SUDS) or *water-sensitive urban design* (WSUD). Storm water is conducted though channels to lagoons situated with a development. From there, it can be released very slowly or be lost through evaporation. Its quality can be managed through appropriate planting regimes. When coupled with planting strategies for the area as a whole for both private and public open space, run-off can be minimised and storm water retained with each development rather than being transferred elsewhere at higher velocity through storm drains. This approach can be taken further using lagoons to treat grey water and, in the most ambitious schemes, black water. The lagoon can also be used to host appropriate flora and fauna to enhance biodiversity.

The sub-goals concerned with energy use, biodiversity and water management come together for the promotion of a *beneficent microclimate*. Planting in urban areas also has significance in terms of microclimate as well as biodiversity. Large trees, supplemented by other soft landscaping, serve to create a favourable microclimate. In rural areas, vegetation and the surrounding soils absorb and retain rainwater, which the heat of the sun then evaporates. The energy from the sun also powers the process of transpiration in plants. Both these processes create a cooling effect. On the other hand, in urban areas, the thermal mass of buildings and paving absorbs the sun's heat in the daytime and releases it at night. This process causes urban areas to be warmer than surrounding rural areas by several degrees (Gilbert, 1991). The creation of planted areas within urban areas can therefore mitigate this effect by converting the heat from the sun into evaporation and transpiration. All the vegetation taken together increases the moisture in the atmosphere. Ponds and other water features can enhance this effect. Large trees provide shade from the sun. They can shade not just people but also the buildings and paving, preventing the absorption of heat from the sun.

All this is in addition to the aesthetic qualities of landscaped areas which fulfil the sub-goal of the need for pleasant, ideally beautiful, surroundings which has a long tradition in the design of liveable cities. The goal of *quality of life* requires provision for open space for healthy physical activities and for quiet relaxation. These will span a wide range of provision and will interact with the perimeter blocks, mentioned above and explained below, in that some will be of a private nature to the rear of buildings and some in public spaces supervised by pedestrian movement and by overlooking. It interacts also with the sub-goal of *promotion of biodiversity*, as already discussed. Appropriate density of planting can also help to support the sub-goal of a beneficial microclimate and reinforces the aesthetic goals through their contribution to townscape.

Pursuit of urban agriculture

In additional to their environmental and recreational roles, green areas in urban areas have a very significant role to play in urban agriculture. As Michael Hough (1989) has explained in some detail, the past history of urban agriculture and future potential is of considerable importance. In most western countries, urban areas now produce little food and this is a declining trend. Most food is sourced from places remote from cities. However, this was not always the case in these same countries, and it is not the case today for most Asian countries. Until at least the early twentieth century, cities in Europe and North America produced significant amounts of food from within their own boundaries. In the early twenty-first century (Hough,

2004), there are major cities in China that are, or nearly are, self-sufficient in vegetables and freshwater fish farmed from land within or immediately adjacent to the city limits. As Hough (1989) explains, there are considerable economic advantages to urban agriculture, not least the lower transport costs, and the sustainability arguments are incontrovertible.

There are at least three types of cultivated urban land – the backyard, the allotment garden and the urban farm. The roles they play can be illustrated well by the example of the British experience during the twentieth century. For historical reasons, back gardens have been a common feature in suburban residential areas in England, if not the rest of Britain, since at least the mid-nineteenth century. During the period between the two world wars, extensive new housing provision for both middle income owner-occupiers and for those renting from local councils was built using a house-and-garden form. The privations of the Second World War encouraged people to put their gardens to good use for food production and this was encouraged strongly by government policy. The growing of vegetables and the keeping of chickens became a nearly universal practice and a proportion kept bees, rabbits and even pigs and goats (Hough, 1989). After the end of the war, such practices declined, and have now largely disappeared, but the point is that it showed what could be done. On the other hand, the use of rented allotments within communal allotment gardens is still a common feature. They were already established by the start of the Second World War and their use expanded greatly during it. Since then, the degree of take up of allotments has varied both between different parts of the country and over time, but they remain a permanent feature.

The last decades of the twentieth century and the first of the twenty-first have showed renewed interest from many quarters, and in many parts of the world, in the potential for urban agriculture (Viljoen and Bohn, 2014). Numerous schemes locally for urban farms, allotments and other forms of cultivated space, both large and small, have been promoted within existing cities. Most often they are initiatives of local people, something that is very welcome and to be encouraged. However, what must also be noted is that, with certain exceptions, they are not part of a general and official planning strategy. In addition, they are, almost exclusively, a matter of retrofitting existing, mainly older, urban environments, especially in cases of urban regeneration. There is no systematic incorporation of provision for urban agriculture in the design of new suburbs or new towns and villages. It is this notable gap in planning and design policy that can be filled by the proposals made in this book.

Overview

What should be noted from the discussion in this chapter is that the importance of setting out goals in a systematic manner is not to arrive eventually at a utopian ideal or to 'give people what they want' but to be better placed to resolve their apparent contradictions. This is at the heart of what planning is all about and its ultimate expression should be as a generator for the physical form of cities. The goals set out here are not, in themselves, unusual and novel. They are, indeed, to be found in most of the writing on social and environmental matters. No really new innovation in values is suggested in the context of most progressive thinking that prevails at the time of writing. This can be illustrated by putting it in the negative. For example, is anyone seriously suggesting that in the long term, energy should be wasted rather than conserved? Similarly, the urban design qualities described are to be found in most texts on planning and design. As was proposed at the beginning of the chapter, the task was to put the relationship of the design of urban form to planning goals on a systematic basis. This was done, though not in pursuit merely of theoretical elegance but for the more practical purpose of improving the layout of cities. The test of whether this has been worthwhile will be the degree to which it can lead to types of form that will not only provide the optimum fulfilment of the goals and sub-goals but also be robust in doing so in the long term.

The argument in this chapter has already started to lead to physical outcomes – an urban form that is medium density and incorporates significant planted open space both public and private. It would have an interconnected grid of roads for movement leading to the form of the perimeter block. It would retain and conserve historic features and attempt to create a sense of place using both old and new. The development of a more detailed typology of the desired urban form will be addressed by the next chapter.

References

Bentley, Ian, Alcock, Alan, Murrain, Paul, McGlynn, Sue and Smith, Graham (1985) *Responsive Environments: A Manual for Designers*, London: Architectural Press.

Cullen, Gordon (1961) *Townscape*, London: The Architectural Press.

Gilbert, O. L. (1991) *The Ecology of Urban Habitats*, London: Chapman and Hall.

Hall, A. C. (1996) *Design Control: Towards a New Approach*, Oxford: Butterworth-Heinemann.

Hall, Peter (2005) *The Land Fetish*, TCPA Tomorrow Series, Paper 16, London: Town and Country Planning Association.

Hough, Michael (1989) *City Form and Natural Process: Towards a New Urban Vernacular*, London: Routledge.

Hough, Michael (2004) *Cities and Natural Process: A Basis for Sustainability*, London: Routledge.

Lynch, Kevin (1960) *The Image of the City*, Cambridge, MA: MIT Press.

Pyšek, Petr (1989) On the richness of central European urban flora, *Preslia*, 61, pp. 329–334.

Viljoen, André and Bohn, Katrin (eds) (2014) *Second Nature Urban Agriculture: Designing Productive Cities*, Abingdon: Routledge.

5 Deriving form
A robust typology

The purpose of the preceding chapter was to set out goals and derive from them the sub-goals and design qualities in a systematic manner. Where there were apparent contradictions between them, this was seen as a creative opportunity to seek a physical solution. Chapter 4 also stressed the need for significant vegetated areas within urban form, both public and private, in pursuit of biodiversity, beneficial microclimate, sustainable management of storm water and urban agriculture, in addition to their central aesthetic and recreational roles. In this chapter the task will be to derive from them types of form that will not only give an optimum fulfilment of the goals and sub-goals but be robust in doing so in the long term.

The perimeter block

The discussion of the quality of *permeability* in Chapter 4 led to one particular type of form, the *perimeter block*. It was illustrated by Figure 4.2. Its value lies in its ability to resolve a number of apparently conflicting sub-goals. It does this through its essential feature, the public front and private back. The public front facilitates access both on foot and for motor vehicles. It encourages sociability and thus security in public. It may be noisy at the front but not necessarily so. The private back gives privacy, security in private and the opportunity for quiet enjoyment. It can also provide for secure play for young children and planting with a considerable degree of biodiversity.

In Europe and North America it has been characteristic of most planned and reconstructed areas of towns and cities since the late eighteenth century because it has been a simple and effective solution. It is true that there were many examples of new residential developments in these same parts of the world during the mid- to late twentieth century where it was not adhered to. However, examination of urban form without it is enough to reveal its advantages. Without it, there is not only poor security but poor aesthetics arising from the exposure of the back of premises to the public realm.

In northern Europe, North America and Australasia there is a strong tradition of private open space around, and especially to the rear, of dwellings. This may take the form of private gardens for family houses or for communal gardens for blocks of flats. It is true that in many other parts of the world perimeter blocks may have little in the way of planted private backs. However, it can be argued that this is to their disadvantage on environmental grounds. In the planned city, vegetation around buildings is important and should occur in both the public and private realms for the reasons that have been argued in Chapter 4.

Issues for building typology

The goals of minimising both energy use and the emission of pollutants lead to criteria for building design:

* minimising energy and pollutants necessary for the occupation of buildings, especially for heating and cooling;
* minimising energy, pollutants and waste products embodied in the manufacture of building materials and construction of buildings, including carbon emissions.

The goal relating to the economic use of land and infrastructure implies the pursuit of development on previously developed land and the reuse of existing buildings. Reuse is not just a matter of retaining existing buildings. There should be the ability to alter and extend the type, mix and quality of activities within a structure while minimising alteration to the building itself and avoiding the need to demolish and replace it, which is known as *robustness*. The term *robustness* was one of the many new terms coined in the book *Responsive Environments* (Bentley et al., 1985) where it was also applied to the design of public spaces, that is, spaces should be designed to facilitate a range of activities and allow them to change over time without significant alteration to the fabric. (In this book, the term has been extended to cover the design of the city as a whole.) The concept has a close relation to the concept of the *extendibility* of buildings, particularly family houses. Whereas this is not appropriate for all buildings, the idea is that it is advantageous if their design allows scope for extending their size with minimal impact on both the original structure and surrounding buildings and spaces.

The goal of economic prudence would lead to the extension or reconstruction of existing infrastructure where this is more economical than rebuild. Were there to be locally underused roads, railways, sewage disposal and water supply facilities then the location of a compact new development should take account of this. However, its most significant implication is for building typology. Robustness can most easily be achieved through *shallow-plan buildings,* as illustrated diagrammatically by Figure 5.1. If a building is short from front to back compared to its length then it can accommodate a range of uses. Shallow-plan structures for new build may be more easily converted at a future date should the need arise. The goal for minimising

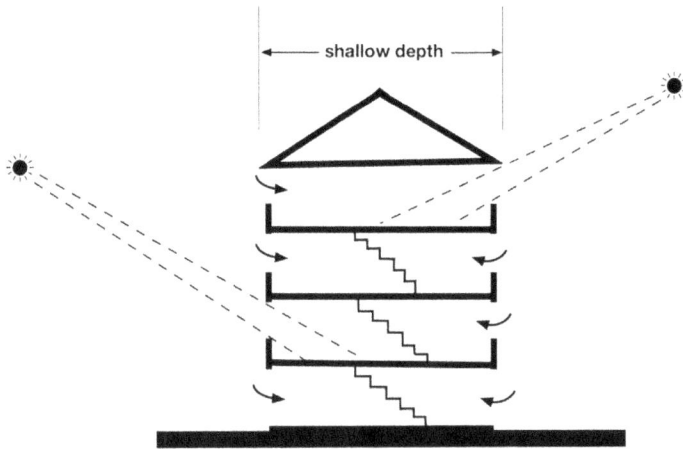

Figure 5.1 The principle of shallow-plan construction. The limited depth of the building allows for natural light and ventilation and is robust in being able to accommodate a range and combinations of uses

Source: Diagram © Tony Hall

the use of energy relates closely to that of the pursuit of the use of renewable energy sources. The criteria leading from this would include the encouragement of buildings that incorporate energy conservation. This also leads to shallow-plan structures as they facilitate natural light and ventilation and to heating and cooling systems designed to conserve energy. Deep-plan structures, whatever their height, cannot be lit and ventilated naturally and thus require electrical energy on a continuous basis for their occupation. On the other hand, shallow-plan structures are not only robust for multiple and changing uses but also for conservation of energy.

The energy required to operate a building, and keep it habitable, goes beyond that needed for lighting, heating and cooling. There is also the operation of lifts and escalators where these are incorporated into the structure. Beyond this *operational*, or *primary*, energy requirement there is also the *embodied* energy of the building. The building materials used its construction, especially concrete, steel, bricks and glass, all have to be manufactured. The manufacturing process consumes considerable quantities of energy and can produce significant quantities of carbon emissions. There is also the energy used in transporting materials to the construction site and erecting the structure. Ultimately, there is also the energy used in the demolition of the building at the end of its lifespan and carrying away the waste materials. These waste materials present additional sustainability issues as, where they cannot be recycled, they would normally go to landfill. This reminds us that, in addition to conservation of energy, there is also a sub-goal of prudent management of building materials. This implies preference for material from renewable sources, that are non-polluting and with minimal implication for waste disposal in the event of demolition, that is, they can be reused or recycled. This can be achieved with the use of lightweight panels made from recycled or renewable materials. As with energy, this argues against the use of steel and concrete and towards guidance for, and limits to, height, with an ideal of two to three storeys and a maximum of four.

Clearly, building technology will change over the long time periods that are stressed in this book. However, one point would seem to be robust over time: the higher the structure, the higher the primary and embodied energy. Up to three storeys, lightweight components of sustainable manufacture can be employed. Above four storeys, steel and concrete are required, and the higher the structure, the more they become essential. Steel and concrete have high embodied energy and high embodied carbon emissions. Above four storeys, lifts are essential with their high daily electrical energy requirements. Again, the higher the building the more essential the use of the lift becomes for the occupants and the higher the energy use. Very tall buildings are difficult to ventilate naturally. Car parking for the occupants needs to be in multi-storey structures which require larger quantities of steel and concrete for their construction than do those for people.

All these arguments lead to a particular building type: shallow plan, two to four storeys. This outcome is supported by research into the life cycle energy characteristics of building types (Norman, MacLean and Kennedy, 2006; Gustavsson and Joelsson, 2010; Fuller and Crawford, 2011) and can be seen in the design of housing in sustainable settlements in Western Europe – two to three storey houses in examples in Britain and the Netherlands and three to four storey apartments in examples in Germany, Scandinavia and Austria.

Density dilemmas

At this point, the reader may be concerned about apparent contradictions between the recommendations for residential density and building types and the objective of minimising energy for travel, particularly by private vehicles. What we seem to be encouraging is low-rise buildings in a green environment with planting in private and public open space to encourage biodiversity, sustainable drainage and a beneficial microclimate. Would this not imply a low-density urban form that would lead to high car use? On the other hand, do not high buildings lead to a high-density form which would encourage low levels of car use? The answer is *not necessarily*. This is also a case of how objectives can be in apparent tension but how this tension can lead to a design solution.

Residential development at very low density, say below 10 dwellings per hectare (dph), can offer its inhabitants advantages in terms of space around the house and a landscape-dominant environment. This may also be good for biodiversity, water management and microclimate. However, this is not necessarily the case in all circumstances. For example, in Australia since the late 1990s, low-density suburbs with little green space between houses and, therefore, none of these advantages have become the norm (Hall, 2010). The main disadvantages are often long distances between houses and local shops, community facilities including schools, and public transport stops as well as between neighbours. These are not beneficial for sociability, security and conservation of energy.

On the other hand, it is possible to have low-density residential areas where houses are within walking distance of public transport. Examples can easily be found from cities in Europe and North America from the early twentieth century where this occurs with low-density suburban form. They were laid out around rail-based transport before the age of high car ownership. Issues of proximity to services can be overcome. The real challenge is the viability of these services. Will there be enough customers to make the provision of public transport, shops and schools economic?

The standard argument for higher residential densities is the converse of all these points. It would mean that services can be located near to dwellings and that such services would be economically viable. Arguments for increased residential densities (Newman and Kenworthy, 1999) have related expenditure of energy on transport to overall population (and job) density for cities around the world. They show that cities with low gross population densities, as in the USA and Australia, have high transport energy use and those with high densities, in Europe and East Asia, have very low usage. As impressive as the statistics are, the method and argument have not been without their critics (Gomez-Ibanez, 1991; Kirwan, 1992; Mindali et al., 2004). The statistics relate to population and employment densities, and also to quantity of public transport, at a macro level rather than the design of cities. Is, however, the argued link causal, and will its converse apply? If new construction is at a higher density, will it automatically be characterised by lower car use? As we have already noted, a walkable neighbourhood centred on a station on a rapid transport line would be expected to facilitate sustainable transport usage irrespective of density. If the design of urban form is studied at the neighbourhood level, there is no particular evidence to suggest that an increase in density within new construction will automatically result in lower energy expenditure irrespective of its design and the way its form relates to the transport infrastructure. The point is that the issue of transport usage cannot be divorced from the design of the urban form of localities.

There are two far more important points that have to be made. First, it must be noted that transport energy is not the only energy that should be conserved. As has already been explained, there is also the energy used to heat or cool buildings and the energy embodied in their construction. At high densities, say above 60 dph and definitely above 100 dph, building heights will all need to be substantially in excess of four storeys and therefore operational and embodied energy will be unavoidably high. Secondly, conservation of energy is only one component of sustainability. There is also the reduction of pollutants, particularly carbon emissions, conservation of water and promotion of biodiversity, a beneficial microclimate, social and recreation activities and their contribution to human health. These are all interrelated with the incorporation of planted areas, which becomes more and more difficult as density increases. Most of these factors are inversely related to residential density: all of them will be affected by the design of urban form. Over and above the sustainability issues, maintenance of sociability and security become more difficult at very high densities where high-rise buildings are required.

What is fortunate is that there is an optimum solution available in terms of a particular type of built form that can resolve the apparent dilemma. As has been noted already, structures of two to four storeys can be naturally lit and ventilated and can be constructed of material with low embodied energy and minimal waste and pollution impacts. With proper design, lifts are not essential at this storey height, reducing operational energy requirements. A further design characteristic can now be introduced, namely the linking of dwellings side-to-side to form terraces or row houses. This is a traditional built form of long-standing because it provides higher density while retaining the advantages of the perimeter block. If properly handled, it can also provide a reduction of heat loss in cold climates. It facilitated the garden city movement precept of 12 houses to an acre or 30 dph (Unwin, 2013). In Britain, this figure was reaffirmed as a target by the 1999 Urban Task Force report (UTF, 1999) and was the government's minimum requirement for new residential development for many years after that. At the corners on the perimeter blocks, flats with communal rear gardens can be used to turn the corners, as illustrated by Figure 5.2. This type of form incorporating low-rise terrace houses with the use of some flats can produce, in practice, residential densities of 25–55 dph (Hall, 2007), and generally around 30 dph. What we have here is an optimal type of urban form emerging from the goals as a resolution of potential conflicts between them.

Issues for streets

Consideration of street design must start with public safety. We have already considered the matter of protection against crime in the public realm in the previous chapter and we must now turn to the issue of conflict between pedestrians, cyclists and motor vehicles. This concern interacts with the sub-goal of reduction of pollution. Measures that involve the control of the movements of motor vehicles for reasons of safety can also be used to ameliorate their polluting effects from noise and gas emissions. The arguments are very similar to those set out for the reduction of crime and protection of privacy.

The general issues relating to the planning for the use of private motor vehicles were set out in Chapter 2. To summarise, the popular approach during the 1960s to 1980s in Europe, North America and elsewhere for

Figure 5.2 Terraced town houses with private rear gardens with the corner of the perimeter block turned by flats with a communal rear garden

Source: Drawn by Matthew Ryan under the direction of the author. © Tony Hall.

dealing with motor traffic was one of separation of land uses. In North America it is still a prevalent approach at the time of writing. This involved separating land devoted to road traffic movement, where there would be little emphasis on environmental quality, from areas where the environmental quality prevailed. Major retail and entertainment facilities were, and are, pedestrianised, often indoors within large structures. There is nothing wrong with pedestrian-only environments as such. The problem has been that, to achieve full car access, they have to be surrounded by extensive areas of roads and car parking which isolate them from other land uses. In residential areas, traffic flows were, and are, curtailed by circuitous routing and the use of cul-de-sacs. Even then full motorisation could not be achieved. The problem was the space taken up by the vehicles in two dimensions. To achieve complete motor vehicle access in city centres would require rebuilding them on many levels. The approach worked, within its own terms of maximising motor vehicle access, for a section of the population on the edge of cities. The problem in applying it within the sustainable city is that it conflicts with the other goals. The area for traffic movement clearly will never meet goals for the pursuit of aesthetics and other aspects of the quality of life. Neither will it meet the sub-goal of being economical with the use of land where it is under pressure. The circuitous and extended cul-de-sac layouts produced within environmental areas do not meet the sub-goal of making it easy to find one's way, nor do they encourage sociability and, from it, security.

On the other hand, the sub-goals of the pursuit of sociability, security and aesthetics can lead to solutions for the detailed design of streets. Places where people can walk freely and safely and enjoy outdoor activities will best be achieved where there is enclosure of space by buildings, that is, the buildings are near together, and where they have active frontages. Whereas this can be achieved fairly easily if streets are for pedestrians only, the scope for such streets on a general basis is limited because of the practical need for motor vehicle access for the delivery of both people and goods. The alternative way of dealing with the danger of vehicles (motor vehicles and, to a lesser extent, cyclists) is by reduction of speed through physical measures, the approach known as *traffic calming*. As was explained in Chapter 2, traffic-calming techniques allow vehicle access to be consistent with social activity in a safe milieu by physically restraining vehicle speed. This implies an urban form with overall traffic speeds below 50 kph, with residential areas at a maximum of 30 kph, often much less. All uses, residential, retail and commercial would have active frontage to the street. By ensuring that vehicle speeds are kept low, pedestrians and vehicles can use the same spaces more safely. This enables active uses to front streets containing motor traffic and the streets to be in a grid form, as follows from the other sub-goals.

It would, however, be unrealistic to imagine people who are seeking a high quality of life being satisfied with low-speed roads as the only means of interurban private travel. The design of wider urban areas must allow for some car travel between settlements at a reasonable speed. There is also the need for provision for the delivery of goods by motor vehicles, in many cases heavy ones. Heavy goods vehicles on roads take up a lot of space, even at low speed, but, more importantly, they have a weight problem. The impact of axle loads upon road surfaces and foundations is proportional to at least the fourth power of the weight. The costs of construction and maintenance of roads able to bear the weight of heavy goods vehicles are, therefore, very high. The dimensions of the same vehicles require, in addition, wider roads and parking bays than would be the case if only cars were involved. The implication of these points for the design of urban form is a two-level road hierarchy for motor vehicles:

- urban streets with low speeds, limitations on heavy vehicles, active frontages and enclosure of space;
- motor roads with higher speeds, surfaces supporting heavy vehicles, no necessary building frontage and restricted access.

These types already exist within the multi-level road hierarchies that are common in traffic engineering and planning throughout the world. The radical suggestion made here is not these two types in themselves, as they already exist, but that there would be nothing in between. It is suggested that it is in the *in-between* situation, where a priority for motor traffic attempts to co-exist with other activities, that the problems in attaining the goals occur. How a two-level hierarchy might be achieved for circulation within cities is discussed in the next two chapters but some points do need to be made here. The principal design challenge is not, in fact, the provision for the private car but for the delivery of goods by road. How much of a settlement can accommodate access by heavy goods vehicles on local roads? Where should *break-bulk*, the transfer of goods from heavy to light vehicles, occur? How can this be designed so that it will be robust over the long lifespan of the urban form? There is also the similar issue of access on local roads, particularly in residential areas, for fire service vehicles and refuse collection. There is also the issue of *park-and-ride* provision – the use of private motor vehicles to park at public transport stops in order to access them. In physical terms, this is not compatible with the location of other uses on, and around, the transit stops because of the space that the cars take up. If *park and ride* is considered essential for reasons of transport policy, then the solution is to have dedicated public transport stops for this activity.

These issues can often be resolved by detailed design at the local level but the more general prescription over wide areas will be addressed in the next chapter. Chapter 6 will also examine how the sub-goal of access is to be pursued if it cannot be achieved through use of the private vehicle as explained both here and in Chapter 2. The proposed solution will be that all activities must be reachable either on foot or by public transport or a combination of both modes. Access on foot also supports the sub-goal of pursuit of recreation and exercise.

Mixing uses

The quality of *mix of use* is the idea that urban activities should, where possible, take place in close proximity to each other and that this should not just be allowed but encouraged. As a design principle this is comparatively recent, historically speaking, coming to the fore only in the late twentieth century. Before then, it might have been seen as a characteristic of the unplanned city, with the planned city characterised by the segregation of land uses. Such segregation has been a practice in planned settlements throughout the ages, and especially so during the mid-twentieth century. Certainly, when dealing with noxious manufacturing activities, it made sense to separate them from other land uses. However, such uses are now rare in post-industrial economies. A more ideological basis came from the modern movement in architecture and was made manifest in new towns and cities in the mid-twentieth century, probably the most famous example being the new capital of Brazil, Brasilia, in the 1960s. In the twentieth century, though, it was not just planning policies that worked to separate land uses into uniform parcels but also commercial pressures. When unconstrained by planning policies, developers may wish to build only those land uses that are most profitable even though they could still make money by building others as well. Whereas segregation of uses is no longer in fashion as a planning idea, it still occurs in contemporary circumstances, because of the continuation of these commercial pressures and the desire to accommodate the needs of unrestrained motor transport, especially the space it requires in two dimensions.

It is important, though, to be very clear about what might be wrong with large areas of single land use and what might be desirable about an integrated mixture. Hopefully, the arguments in this book can lend clarity to the debate. The sub-goal of seeking minimisation of the use of energy leads to a hierarchy of locational criteria for development giving priority to proximity of activities as far as possible. The sub-goals of the pursuit of a safe and sociable environment also lead to provision of public areas with a strong mix of activities. This can be very important for less mobile members of the community, such as the very young and very old. It also adds to the overall richness and enjoyability of the urban environment. It may be difficult to require multiple uses in all cases, especially in residential areas, as it may be that economic and social forces do not support them. What, however, would be incompatible with the goals set out in this book would be any type of form exhibiting complete segregation of land uses in two dimensions in such a way that it prevented a future mixing of uses.

Summary

To summarise, we have arrived at desired types of urban form which possess certain defined characteristics. Their relationship to the goals is set out in Table 5.1. For urban areas that are primarily residential and commercial, the outcomes would be characterised by the following features:

- perimeter blocks;
- pedestrian scale with most local activities within walking distance;
- public transport within walking distance;
- grid road layout with minimal use of cul-de-sacs;
- motor vehicle access to properties but at slow speed;
- active frontage to streets;
- mixed uses;
- public realm enclosed by buildings or trees creating varied spaces;
- parks, and other green spaces of varied nature, within walking distance.

For buildings:

- shallow plan;
- construction from sustainable materials;
- generally two to four storeys, maximum five.

Table 5.1 Interrelationship between sub-goals and characteristics of urban form

	Beautiful surroundings	Security	Privacy	Quietude	Sociability	Access	Finding the way	Recreation and exercise	Water usage minimisation	Energy usage minimisation	Biodiversity maximisation	Land economy	Sustainable materials	Pollution minimisation
Perimeter blocks		•	•	•	•		•							
Pedestrian scale	•				•			•		•				•
Public transport					•	•				•				
Grid road layout		•			•	•	•							
Slow vehicle access					•					•				•
Active frontage	•	•			•	•	•							
Mixed uses					•	•	•			•		•		
Public realm enclosure	•						•							
Parks and green spaces	•			•	•			•	•	•	•			•
Shallow plan										•			•	
Sustainable materials										•			•	•
Two to five storeys, maximum five										•			•	
Terraced										•		•		
Medium density					•					•	•	•		
Rear gardens	•	•	•	•				•	•			•		•

Residential areas would be:

- medium density – 20–60 dph;
- predominantly terraced houses, often with some flats integrated into the design;
- have rear gardens or other private space.

There will be other areas, such as those characterised by manufacturing and distribution activities, and those lying between urban areas, where motor roads without active frontage and higher vehicle speeds would apply.

In contrast, urban form that exhibited the following characteristics would not be consistent with the precepts advanced in this chapter:

- high-rise;
- concrete and steel frame construction;
- uninhabitable without air conditioning;
- little enclosure of space by building and/or trees;
- extensive surfaces impermeable to water;
- lack of urban vegetation;
- lack of active frontage;
- dependent on the motor vehicle for access;
- excessive use of cul-de-sacs;
- exposure of private rear boundaries;
- excessive segregation of land uses.

Relationship to past and current practice

To what extent does this compare with past and current practice? The physical outcomes advocated here can trace an ancestry back to at least the late nineteenth century, if not further. There are examples on the ground and they have been lived and worked on for many generations. This type of form can be seen, for example, in historic continuity in English practice. It was seen first in the late nineteenth century in the ideal settlements built by a few enlightened industrialists for their employees as, for example, at Bournville, Port Sunlight and New Earswick. It emerged in force in the garden city movement and the first garden cities at Letchworth and Welwyn. It could also be seen in same period at Hampstead Garden Suburb and the cottage estates in the social housing schemes following the First World War. In a somewhat debased form it continued in the social housing estates built in the 1930s and 1950s. These examples sometimes incorporated a limited use of cul-de-sacs but not to the extent to call into question the general approach to layout. Cul-de-sacs also featured in the *Essex Design Guide* of 1973 (Essex County Council, 1973) as it was about the only legal way of restraining traffic flow at the time. However, apart from this, this guide represented a forceful restatement of the type of form recommended here. It was applied to private housing and the results can be seen in many housing schemes in Essex built according to this guide. A fully revised version was published in 1997 (Essex County Council, 2005). Cul-de-sacs were no longer recommended and the desirability of terraced houses and gardens enclosing urban streets was re-emphasised. Numerous schemes were subsequently built across the county according to the precepts of the revised Essex guide (Hall, 2007). The 1990s also saw the construction of the first phases of the now famous extension to the city of Dorchester known as Poundbury (Hardy, 2006), which also emphasised the same approach.

The turn of the twentieth–twenty-first centuries saw the publication of a number of national policy guides (DETR, 1998, 2000; DTLR and CABE, 2001; Llewelyn Davies, English Partnerships and the Housing Corporation, 2000, 2007; DCLG and DoT, 2007) all recommending what had become progressive urban design thinking and practice. This advice, together with a government policy for a minimum density of 30 dph in new housing schemes, was reflected in the publication of a large number of local design guides and influenced the construction of exemplars throughout the country. One notable characteristic of English practice, when compared to other countries, has been the use of neo-vernacular styles. Houses mimic the architecture of rural towns and villages, and other traditional urban styles, and employ building materials characteristic of the area in pursuit of a local sense of place.

For much of the twentieth century, new suburban housing in the Netherlands also followed a medium-density, terraced house-and-garden form, although the use of traditional styles has been more restrained than in England. From the 1990s onwards, modernist designs were more in evidence although the house-and-garden form has still been retained. This was characteristic not just of sustainable development showpieces, such as Ecolonia at Alphen aan den Rijn, but also of new mass housing developments on the outskirts of many Dutch cities. At the same time it is true that, for complex historical reasons that need not detain us here, the predominant residential provision in many European cities during the nineteenth and early twentieth centuries was in the form of apartment blocks, typically six storeys, arranged in perimeter blocks within a grid of formal streets, rather than family houses. Such traditions have been reflected in many new developments from the early twenty-first century that have been regarded as sustainable exemplars, such as Hammarby Sjöstad in Stockholm, Solar City outside Linz in Austria and the urban extensions of Rieselfeld and Vauban to Freiburg im Breisgau in Germany where flats and town houses have been used but with the building heights generally limited to four to five storeys. However, what is notable, especially in Freiburg, is the presence of private gardens for ground-level dwellings and terraces and balconies for flats. At the same time there has been ample provision of planted public open space, and car usage, although allowed, is significantly restrained.

The important example from North America is *New Urbanism*. It emerged in the USA during the late 1980s and early 1990s. It represented a rejection by a number of concerned architects and planners of the low-density, car-based suburban development surrounding North American cities and also of modernist approaches to higher-density development. A group who were to become its leading protagonists formed the *Congress for New Urbanism* (CNU) in 1991. They subsequently published the *Charter of the New Urbanism* which was later made available as an edited book (CNU, 2000). The charter saw a primary task of all urban architecture and landscape design to be the physical definition of streets and public spaces as places of shared use, integrated with their surroundings. Architecture and landscape design should grow from local climate, topography, history and building practice. All buildings should provide their inhabitants with a clear sense of location, weather and time. Natural methods of heating and cooling should be promoted. The charter contained a long list of principles but those that affect the argument of this book are those relating to the idea of *traditional neighbourhood development*. They promoted walkable neighbourhoods which were to be compact, pedestrian-friendly and mixed use. Many activities of daily living should occur within walking distance, allowing independence to those who do not drive. Interconnected networks of streets should be designed to encourage walking, reduce the number and length of car trips, and conserve energy. There should be a range of parks. A broad range of housing types and price levels should bring people of diverse ages, races and incomes into daily interaction.

Unfortunately, there is a problem when analysing New Urbanist practice: that of too few examples. Regrettably, the design of most suburban *sprawl* in North America has continued as before. However, the examples that are recognised by most American New Urbanists as characteristic, such as Kentland, Maryland, and Cherry Hill, Michigan, show the characteristics of form set out in the charter. It can be argued that New Urbanism exhibits a close correspondence with many of the key aspects of English practice (Tiesdell, 2002). They are not quite as high a density as the European examples nor do they put the same emphasis on private gardens but they do share with English practice the emphasis on traditional form and style. What has become, though, an almost defining characteristic of New Urbanist housing schemes has been the emphasis on removing cars from the streets at the front of the houses over and above other design considerations. The vehicles are accommodated in rear lanes and parking courts even to the extent of compromising the security of the private backs of the perimeter blocks

New Urbanism found a second home in Australia as this country shares the car-based, low-density *sprawl* with North America and, consequently, the reaction to it in certain quarters. Australia did, in fact, have a tradition of nineteenth-century medium-density terraced housing in the cities of Sydney and Melbourne, although construction of this type of form was not pursued during the twentieth century (Freestone, 2010). As in the US, there is a shortage of appropriate examples. There is one twenty-first century example that does have New Urbanist inspired dwellings, Joondalup, north of Perth, with terraced houses reminiscent, in outward appearance, of the late nineteenth-century suburbs of Sydney. These houses, though, have no backyard at all (Hall, 2010).

Nevertheless, there is one circumstance where there is a divergence between the recommendations made here and an aspect of current practice that is aimed at sustainable solutions. This is in the application of the goals – high-rise residential and commercial buildings in and around city centres. High-rise structures would be at odds with the goals and qualities set out here because of their high level of operational and embodied energy use. However, they are seen as a sustainable option in and around city centres by some academic and professional authors and in the practice in some cities (the Canadian city of Vancouver, British Columbia, would be a notable example) because of the way they could reduce the need to travel through very high concentrations of dwellings and activities. The issue is whether or not it is acceptable to obtain a high degree of satisfaction of one goal at the expense of another. The lesson from much European practice is that at residential densities of 30–60 dph and buildings of three to five storeys in height it is possible to achieve optimum solutions with all goals satisfied to a high degree without recourse to very high buildings.

Aside from this particular debate, however, what is remarkable is that all these examples have a very high degree of commonality. The different concepts, theories and areas of technical knowledge that underlie, and have given rise to, urban design thinking since at least the late 1980s all contribute to similar outcomes in terms of type of urban form. There is a general pattern of low-speed grids of streets with restraint of car use and active frontage for streets. Buildings are either two to three storey houses or four to five storey flats with great emphasis on both public and private green space. All the urban design qualities pursued pull together, overlap and reinforce each other. The same goes for their theoretical underpinnings. If it had been the case that, for example, townscape, space syntax and urban morphology all pulled in different directions then choices would have to be made between them. Fortunately, they all tend to roughly the same outcomes.

References

Bentley, Ian, Alcock, Alan, Murrain, Paul, McGlynn, Sue and Smith, Graham (1985) *Responsive Environments: A Manual for Designers*, London: Architectural Press.
CNU, Congress for New Urbanism (2000) *Charter of the New Urbanism*. New York: McGraw-Hill.
DCLG and DoT (2007) *Manual for Streets*, London: Thomas Telford.
DETR (1998) *Planning for Sustainable Development: Towards Better Practice*, London: DETR.
DETR (2000) *Our Towns and Cities: The Future – Delivering an Urban Renaissance*, London: HMSO.
DTLR and CABE (2001) *By Design – Better Places to Live*, London: Thomas Telford.
Essex County Council (1973) *A Design Guide for Residential Areas*, Chelmsford: Essex County Council.
Essex County Council (2005) *The Essex Design Guide*, Chelmsford: Essex County Council, (a reprint of Essex Planning Officers Association (1997) *A Design Guide for Residential and Mixed Use Areas*).
Freestone, Robert (2010) *Urban Nation: Australia's Planning Heritage*, Melbourne: CSIRO Publishing.
Fuller, R. J. and Crawford, R. H. (2011) Impact of past and future residential housing development patterns on energy demand and related emissions, *Journal of Housing and the Built Environment*, 26, pp. 165–183.
Gomez-Ibanez, J. A. (1991) A global view of automobile dependence, *Journal of the American Planning Association*, 57(3), p. 376.

Gustavsson, L. and Joelsson, A. (2010) Life cycle primary energy analysis of residential buildings, *Energy and Buildings*, 42, pp. 210–220.

Hall, Tony (2007) *Turning a Town Around: A Pro-active Approach to Urban Design*, Oxford: Blackwell.

Hall, Tony (2010) *The Life and Death of the Australian Backyard*, Melbourne: CSIRO Publishing.

Hardy, Dennis (2006) *Poundbury, the Town That Charles Built*, London: TCPA.

Kirwan, Richard (1992) Urban Form, Energy and Transport: A Note on the Newman-Kenworthy Thesis, *Urban Policy and Research*, 10(1), pp. 6–23.

Llewelyn Davies, English Partnerships and the Housing Corporation (2000) *Urban Design Compendium Volume 1*, London: English Partnerships and the Housing Corporation.

Llewelyn Davies, English Partnerships and the Housing Corporation (2007) *Designing Quality Places, Urban Design Compendium Volume 2*, London: English Partnerships and the Housing Corporation.

Mindali, O., Raveh, A. and Salomon, I. (2004) Urban Density and Energy Consumption: A New Look at Old Statistics, *Transportation Research Part A*, 38, pp. 143–162.

Newman, Peter and Kenworthy, Jeffrey (1999) *Sustainability and Cities: Overcoming Automobile Dependence*, Washington, DC: Island Press.

Norman, J., MacLean, M. and Kennedy, C. A. (2006) Comparing High and Low Residential Density: Life-Cycle Analysis of Energy Use and Greenhouse Gas Emissions, *Journal of Urban Planning and Development*, 132(1), pp. 10–21.

Tiesdell, Steven (2002) The New Urbanism and English Residential Design Guidance: A Review. *Journal of Urban Design*, 7(3), pp. 353–376.

Unwin, Raymond (2013) *Nothing Gained by Overcrowding*, reprint of the 1910 pamphlet for the Garden Cities and Town Planning Association with an introduction by Mervyn Miller, Studies in International Planning History, Abingdon: Routledge.

UTF, Urban Task Force (1999) *Towards an Urban Renaissance*, London: E & F N Spon.

6 Beads on a string

The purpose of the next two chapters is to explore the implications of the content of the preceding ones for whole city form by means of a theoretical model. It is not suggested that urban form would be laid out precisely as pictured in the diagrams illustrating these chapters. The function of the model will be to test the qualities and criteria proposed and to explore their consequences for urban form in general. The reader will discover that such a model demonstrates that an internally consistent settlement design is possible and that this design has implications for city form that may not have been previously apparent. It also helps to emphasise those parameters that determine the long-term physical structure compared with those that may vary in the shorter term, such as residential density.

Derivation of the ped-shed

Continuing the argument developed in Chapter 5, taking the goals and sub-goals described there and their implications for the design of urban form, the next stage in the process will be to attempt to derive from them more specific locational criteria. The intention is that these criteria would be usable as practical planning principles for the location of development. It will be shown that they imply specific types of urban form.

The goal of *prudent conservation of resources* led to the sub-goal of *minimising use of energy*. It can be argued that this in turn leads to a planning criterion that activities should be located such as to minimise the need to travel. This then leads on to a sequence of further criteria, arranged in order of priority and feasibility of implementation. The logical consequence to be deduced as a first priority would be *no travel*. In practice this would imply no more movement than would be expected within a building or between adjacent buildings. The planning quality following from this is *mixed uses on site*. A definite quantitative criterion for the area of location would be required in practice. This would likely be in tens of metres and a maximum radius of, say, 100 m. In other words, land uses would be immediately adjacent to each other in two dimensions or overlay each other in three dimensions. As stressed in Chapter 5, mixed uses represent a design quality that also stems from the pursuit of the goals of quality of life and is one that is now widely accepted in planning and design circles.

Obviously, not all activities could, or should, be located so close together. Parks and playing fields would not fit and an attempt to combine retail, commercial and residential activities within an excessive extension of three-dimensional megastructures would militate against *quality of life* goals. As a second priority, therefore, urban form should permit uses to be located within walking distance of each other. Again, a quantitative criterion is required. A walking distance can vary between 300 m and 700 m in length, and a typical length is 400 m. A maximum radius of 400 m could be used. Its feasibility would depend upon the economics of development, economics of public transport provision and the minimum thresholds for primary schools. However, if we wish to talk about an absolute maximum for the extent of development, and to explore its consequences for urban form in general, we will need a robust figure that would not normally be exceeded. Urban design guidelines (Llewelyn Davies, English Partnerships and the Housing Corporation, 2000) commonly suggest an average of 400 m and maximum of 800 m radius. The 800 m maximum distance is the figure that will be used here, although the implications of a more typical 400 m distance will also be referred to.

A question that is sometimes asked is why not use cycling distance? The difficulty with such a proposal is that the distances people could cycle are much longer than for walking and could be comparable with those for short car trips. The distance could also vary significantly between different individuals and groups. Even with favourable topography, there are differences in usage dependent upon age and health. There are also the matters of culture and tradition. The very high degree of usage found in the Netherlands and Denmark is well known but it cannot be found in most other developed countries at the time of writing. Without such a strong cycling culture, the danger is that separating development by long cycling distances would, instead, lead to greater car use. On the other hand, walking is something that is open to all but a small minority of people and the special transport facilities for those unable to walk would be likely to lead to a similar scale of provision.

An 800 m maximum radius settlement, or *ped-shed*, is therefore proposed. This term is a rather ugly one but is found in the technical literature and no suitable alternative that is problem free is, unfortunately, currently available. *Neighbourhood* is value-loaded and is discussed later in this chapter. *Township* is similarly problematic because of South African associations. *Settlement* is too general, although it will be used later in this book in places where its generality is appropriate. The structure of a typical 800 m radius ped-shed is illustrated diagrammatically by Figure 6.1.

The ped-shed could be seen as also pursuing the sub-goal of economic use of land where competition for it is strong, through the promotion of

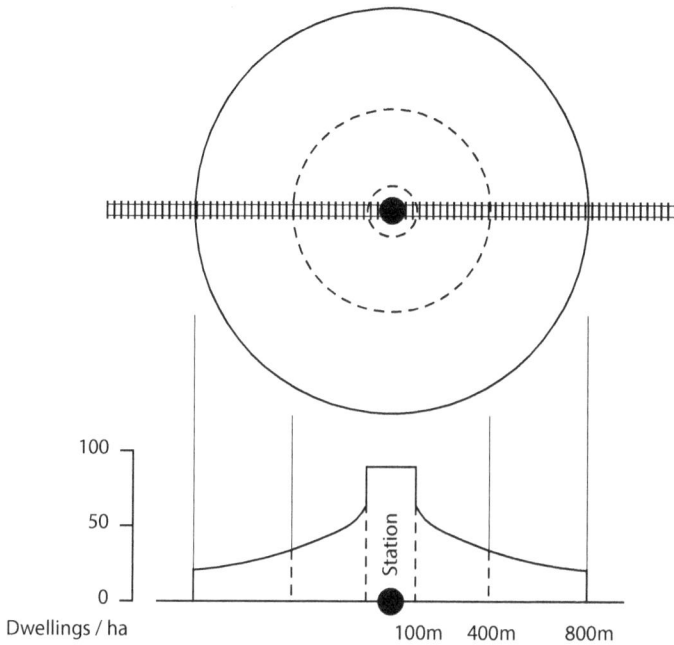

Figure 6.1 The 800 m ped-shed showing a possible gradient of residential density from a mixed-use core around a centrally located station

Source: Drawn by Matthew Ryan under the direction of the author. © Tony Hall.

compact settlements. Because of both the desire to minimise the need to travel and the likely economic pressures on the supply and value of land, the residential density can be expected to decrease with distance from the centre. The absolute levels of residential density would be determined by the distance of the ped-shed as a whole from other urban centres and the socio-economic pressure that would result from this. The levels shown in the diagram, of 100 dph in the 100 m radius central core and a range of 50–20 dph outside it, are just examples, although not untypical ones. Non-residential uses permitted in the settlement would be expected to be concentrated in the mixed-use core where uses may overlay in three dimensions. However, a few non-residential uses might extend beyond this. As we are talking about the long-term physical form rather than the activities within it, there is no reason to preclude other uses such as corner shops, child care facilities and small-scale health care, such doctors' and dentists' surgeries, from being elsewhere within the ped-shed. They are still going to be within walking distance for local residents.

Linking up ped-sheds

There are clearly limits to what facilities could be contained within one 800 m radius settlement. Adoption of a maximum distance implies that once such a settlement has been constructed, this distance cannot be exceeded so a further development would require additional ped-sheds. The goal of pursuit of sustainability now requires, as the third level of priority, that walking gives way to travel by a mode of transport connecting the centres of the ped-sheds but not dependent on the private motor vehicle. This implies that the settlements should be linked by a high-grade public transport corridor, ideally a frequent-service, fixed-track facility. The fixed requirement would be for a public transport stop at the centre of the mixed-use core. This creates what is often known as the *beads-on-string* form as illustrated diagrammatically by Figure 6.2. If a facility is not within walking distance, then it is reachable

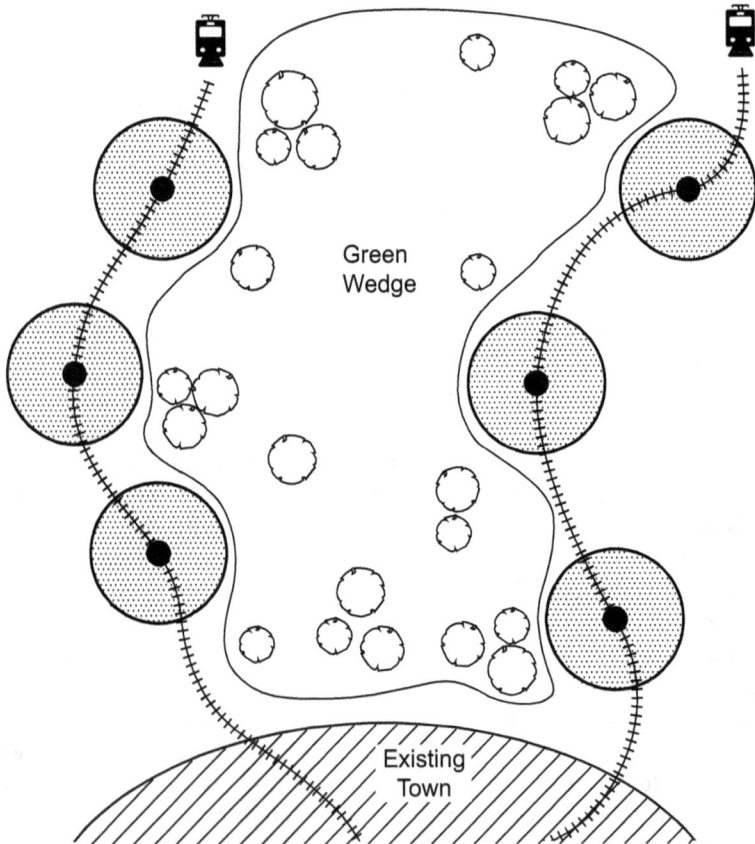

Figure 6.2 Beads-on-string form. The ped-sheds are linked by a quality, track-based public transport line

Source: Drawn by Matthew Ryan under the direction of the author. © Tony Hall.

by walking combined with public transport. Although travel in total is not minimised, the form adopted means that it can still take place in the most energy efficient manner. Note that the form does not necessarily compel the use of walking and public transport but that it does ensure that anyone without private motor transport is not disadvantaged.

The standard of quality proposed here would imply that the public transport services would be *track-based*. *Track-based* could include busways, with or without guided bus technology. A track-based system has the advantage of providing higher capacity, speed and acceleration than public road-based bus services. On the other hand, it also has a higher capital cost and cannot be relocated in response to short-term changes in patterns of demand. However, the difficulty of relocation can be seen as an advantage. It is a fundamental argument of this book that built form lasts a very long time. If there is to be a core transport infrastructure that will support sustainable built form, then this must last an equally long time. Buses services running on public roads can be withdrawn easily and for the type of form proposed here to be built and then lose its service would defeat the whole intention. There are also the added advantages for the track-based system in that it makes it easier for people to find their way and plan their journeys and also that higher income groups will tend to use them in circumstances where they would never use a bus. They attract all sections of society. However, it is not suggested that the existence of track-based systems would exclude provision of other road-based bus services, quite the contrary, and the parallel provision of local bus services is both likely and desirable. They would provide a means of responding to short-term changes in demand as a result of changing urban activities, as opposed to more static urban form. For the main service, though, we are talking about busways, guided bus, light rail or heavy rail services.

Green space in and around the ped-shed

Chapters 4 and 5 have argued for the need for green spaces within the urban area as private gardens and other planted areas around buildings, as local parks, as larger parks and as playing fields. All of these types of provision have their own role – an increased amount in one cannot compensate for deficiencies in the others. Such planted areas within cities are important, not just for recreation, but also for their ecological role in the management of storm drainage, microclimate and biodiversity. They are necessary for dealing with storm water and also advantageous for the processing of wastewater, both grey water and sewage. They also possess substantial cultural and educational value and can play an important role in local food production.

However, not all such provision will fit within an 800 m radius, especially larger playing fields (for educational, private and public use), urban forests and large areas of parkland. These can be located around the edge of each ped-shed and between the strings of them. An additional, and beneficial, result of limiting development to within the 800 m maximum radius is that open land would surround each *bead* and would be within walking distance of all dwellings. This would not only minimise travel to outdoor recreation but also make it available to those without access to a car, especially children. The green areas between the *strings* could be substantial and would not only allow ample room for recreation but would also promote biodiversity and a high level of general amenity.

Chapter 4 explained how, in addition to their environmental and recreational roles, urban green areas would have a very significant role to play in urban agriculture. It was pointed out that there are at least three types of cultivated urban land – the backyard, the allotment garden and the urban farm. As mentioned Chapter 4, in recent decades there have been many examples in cities throughout the world of schemes to establish urban agriculture by these means (Viljoen and Bohn, 2014). They have generally been the initiatives of local people, something quite laudable, and have often been features of urban regeneration. However, this amounted to retrofitting of existing urban form and they are rarely a feature of systematic official planning policy. They have not formed part of the design of urban extensions and new settlements, much less the form of standard car-based suburbs. The idea of having a ped-shed surrounded by a green area can be very useful in developing such policy. Viljoen and Bohn (2014) have argued for what they term *continuous productive urban landscapes,* effectively green corridors constructed through existing urban areas providing primarily for urban agriculture but also for recreation. The principle of a biological continuity between planted areas is an important one and it is facilitated by the beads-on-string arrangement for new development.

As well as the continuity of green space, the finite limit to development at the ped-shed boundary is also important. What can occur in practice, but unfortunately receives little publicity, is a phenomenon that is a largely unintended consequence of green belts, growth boundaries and similar policies: they create a permanent hard edge to built-up areas. The shape and size of these areas where development is not permitted may mean that very large farms may not be economic there. What can happen is that it enables smallholdings to locate adjacent to urban areas. Their market gardening can provide high-value produce for sale directly to shoppers from the adjoining residential areas. Local people can buy from *farm shops* on the smallholdings and the growers can take their produce to local *farmers markets*. An example is shown in Figure 6.3. It shows land between Purley and Banstead on the southern edge of Greater London. The development boundary is created by the Metropolitan Green Belt. The large area occupied by smallholdings is indicated. The author's parents lived for many years in the adjacent residential area and used the farm shops regularly for the purchase of fruit, vegetables and eggs. Their existence is closely linked to local planning policies and other regulations. The smallholders' farm shops are allowed to sell only their own produce.

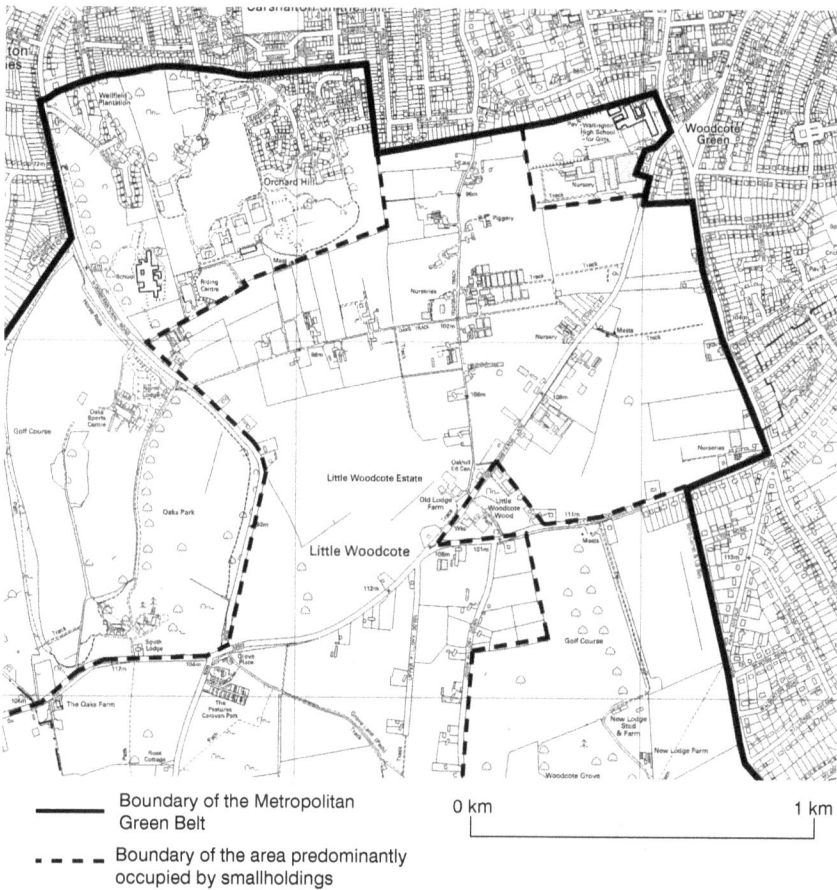

Boundary of the Metropolitan
Green Belt

- - - - Boundary of the area predominantly
occupied by smallholdings

0 km   1 km

Figure 6.3 Area of smallholdings between Purley and Banstead, UK, adjacent to the southern edge of the Greater London urban area and within the Metropolitan Green Belt

Source: Diagram © Tony Hall. Base map reproduced by permission of the Ordnance Survey on behalf of HSMO. © Crown Copyright 2014 Ordnance Survey 100048184. All rights reserved..

However, the long-term issue for the design of urban form is not whether or not most people use particular areas for agriculture at particular points in time but whether this use should be ruled out in perpetuity by failing to provide space for the activity. Unfortunately, the general circumferential growth of cities does not normally provide for urban farms and new allotment gardens and in some parts of the world there may also be little in planted private space around new dwellings. On the other hand, if open land within cities is left un-built on, as is a consequence of the *beads-on-string form*, there is always scope for substantial urban agriculture.

The design of road and rail provision

In order to address the question of the nature of road and rail access to the ped-sheds in more detail, it is helpful to deal separately with the movement of people and with goods. Turning first to the design of roads for the movement of people, the discussion in Chapter 5 established a two-level hierarchy of *frontage access* and *no frontage access* for both pedestrians and vehicles. Within the ped-sheds, motor vehicle access would be permitted but a low-speed environment would favour safe and pleasant movement by foot and bicycle. All the roads, therefore, should have frontage access and speed limited to a maximum of 50 kph or, in some neighbourhoods, 30 kph. The public transport line running through to the station at the centre of the ped-shed could be elevated, placed in a cutting or even put underground, minimising severance of potential pedestrian and vehicle pathways. If the public transport is in the form of trams (streetcars) then they could run on a central reservation on a 50 kph road. In any event, a twin-track, rail-based public transport system would have a narrower width than a major road traffic artery. Local buses within 50 kph roads could supplement the public transport provision both within and between ped-sheds. Such bus provision would be essential for those unable to walk any significant distance.

Higher-speed roads with no frontage access, that is, motorways, would be located outside the ped-sheds and would permit vehicle speeds up to, or even in excess of, 100 kph. They would link the ped-sheds and could carry higher-speed long distance buses in addition to private cars. Higher-speed rail services would also be located outside ped-sheds.

Park-and-ride facilities around public transport stops pose a particular problem. The space taken up by the parking of cars is in conflict with the principle of bringing other uses closer together with pedestrian access. This can be the case even when the parking is multi-storey. Although the commuters arriving at the beginning, and leaving at the end of, the day may bring trade to any adjoining shops at those times, the parking spaces they take up will not be available to customers for the shops coming and going throughout the day. It follows that park-and-ride facilities cannot be combined with the mixed-use provision around station stops at the centres of ped-sheds and would need to be located outside ped-sheds around dedicated public transport stops. This would have the further advantage of allowing direct access by the higher-speed roads.

The transport of goods is not so amenable to such a neat solution. The problem caused by larger vehicles for the delivery of goods is not just their physical dimensions, which can be very intrusive, but also their axle-weight. Axle-weight has an exponential relationship with the impact on the road surface. This means that roads supporting heavy vehicles have substantially higher construction and maintenance costs than if they were built solely for the use of light vehicles such as private cars. It is normal practice for motorways to be designed for use by heavy goods vehicles as well as private cars. Warehouses, and other distribution facilities, would, therefore, need to be outside the ped-sheds and connected directly to motorways. The level of employment in comparison to the size of the facilities is low but, nevertheless, they do employ people and the employees should have the opportunity to get to work by quality public transport. There is, therefore, an argument for locating distribution centres in the same way as park-and-ride facilities – outside ped-sheds but with their own public transport stop. If they were located on the edge of a ped-shed then this would facilitate break-bulk operations whereby freight is transferred from heavy to light vehicles for onward delivery to within the ped-shed. Such facilities are rare at the time of writing because of the significant extra cost of these operations. However, the point here is that the physical arrangement would permit the legal restriction, or even prohibition, of heavy goods vehicles within the ped-shed.

The same arguments relating to the transport of goods by road apply to transport by rail. Freight lines have to be able to cope with heavier axle loads and larger loading gauges than apply on suburban passenger lines. In new construction, they would be separate from the public transport lines and outside the ped-sheds but would serve distribution centres. (The same would apply to the transport of goods by waterways.) However, where existing passenger and freight services shared the same track this arrangement would not be as environmentally disruptive as it would be for road transport and could remain.

Returning to the situation inside the ped-shed, in the absence of a break-bulk facility for the transfer to small, light goods vehicles, there is still a design challenge in achieving an environmentally satisfactory means of delivering goods to the shops and for some of the services to dwellings. A skeletal network of 50 kph roads suitable for use by heavy goods vehicles would be needed to reach the central mixed-use core of the ped-shed even if heavy goods vehicles were restricted in other parts.

Non-residential ped-sheds

It has thus been established that warehouse and distribution centres and park-and-ride facilities should be located outside the residential ped-sheds. The same would go for all other space-hungry, low-intensity commercial and manufacturing uses. The same may also go for very large hospital and educational complexes and they, like park-and-ride facilities, should have their own stop on the quality public transport network. In some cases, they could be sited outside the ped-sheds with their own dedicated station stop. This might be appropriate for some park-and-ride facilities. However, the argument leads to having in some, but not all, circumstances, a non-residential ped-shed containing a combination of such uses, as illustrated diagrammatically by Figure 6.4. Such ped-sheds would be placed at intervals along the public transport line between the residential ped-sheds.

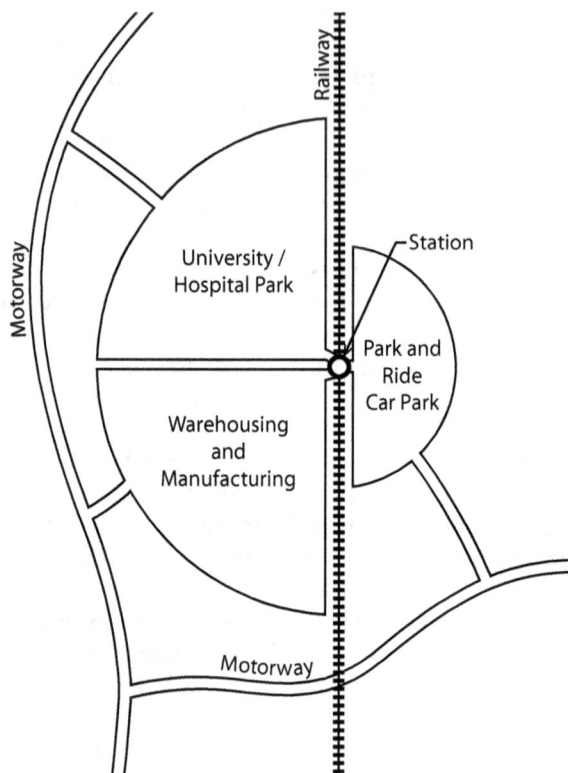

Figure 6.4 A diagrammatic representation of a ped-shed devoted to non-residential uses with a high level of use of, and access for, motor vehicles. In practice, all three of the land uses shown would not necessarily be present together and there may be other possible uses that are not shown

Source: Drawn by Matthew Ryan under the direction of the author. © Tony Hall.

It would also be possible to have a ped-shed that was, say, half non-residential and half residential, or similar proportions. For example, one could contain a large-scale hospital complex, perhaps 400–600 m across, together with an adjacent university campus of similar dimensions and still have nearly half the ped-shed predominantly residential. Moreover, these uses would be compatible, particularly with regard to local employment opportunities. The important point is that the concept is flexible, in other words *robust*, and that the non-residential uses would always be within walking distance of the station on the public transport network.

A corollary of this proposal is the question of which non-residential uses should then be located inside the predominantly residential ped-sheds. It must be emphasised that not all ped-sheds would be the same. Variation in non-residential uses could be expected spatially, affected by degree of proximity to major centres, and, over time, affected by changing market and technological conditions. For example, some may contain major retail centres while others have only a minimum of local shops. Nevertheless, as indicated in the derivation of the ped-shed concept at the beginning of this chapter, the mixed-use core around the public transport station would generally be expected to contain a range of shops, offices for legal and financial services, bars and restaurants, community facilities and health centres. Within the ped-shed, but not necessarily at its centre, would be primary schools, doctor and dental surgeries, convenience stores and local parks and play areas.

Ped-shed spacing

The next question to be addressed is the spacing between the centres of the ped-sheds, that is, the principal stations on the public transport line. The technical literature does not, unfortunately, provide ready-made and packaged, let alone fixed-quantity, answers. The reason for this is a perfectly rational one – there are very many variables involved and a significant proportion of these are value-based, in other words, policy dependent. White (2009) is one of the most helpful sources and does provide a mathematical formula. By inserting typical values for nine variables, he calculates an optimal spacing of stops of 565 m on a track-based system. His value for the vehicle running speed is 43 kph and it is clear that he is discussing a tram (streetcar) operation. Walker (2012) presents a very clear and accessible discussion of distances between public transport stops for bus and tram operation. Assuming a 400 m walking distance (the typical rather than the maximum value used here) he points out that a 400 m stop spacing would produce overlaps in walking distance catchments maximising access opportunities but be more expensive to operate and less useful to riders through slower overall operating speeds. On the other hand, no overlap of walking catchments, and/or the assumption of longer walking distances, would result in greater stop spacing and a speedier service but reduced accessibility for those who are less mobile. He notes that European guidance is a 600 m spacing and actual practice can be 200–400 m for local services.

For the ped-shed spacing, however, we are talking about *quality track-based public transport* not local buses (although bus services would also be provided). The intention, realised in the next chapter, is to construct a model on a citywide scale which would require higher speeds and convenient journey times over longer distances. This is more akin to suburban and underground railways than to buses and trams running on-street. To get a feel of the typical distance between stations they were measured by the author for the track-based systems in a selection of cities around the world. The results are shown in Table 6.1. Generally, the pattern is one of 0.5–1 km gaps in, and near, city centres lengthening to spacing of 1–2 km further out. The Brisbane busways of the early 2000s and the outer parts of the older BART system in San Francisco have spacing in excess of 2 km but serve very low-density suburban areas. (The Paris RER lines also have 2+ km spacings

Table 6.1 Station spacings in selected major cities. Distances in km

	Underground railway	Suburban railway	Other
London	Inner 1.0; outer 1.7–2.0	1.5–2.0	
Manchester		1.0–2.5	Tram 0.7–1.2
Berlin	0.5–1.2	0.8–1.3	
Paris	0.25–0.5m	0.8–1.8	RER 1.7–2.7
Stockholm	Inner 0.5–0.8; outer up to 1.6	1.9–4.7	
Vienna	0.5–1.1	1.3–2.9	Suburban tram 0.2–0.4
Moscow	1.0–4.0; average 1.7	1.5–3.2	
Tokyo	0.6–1.0	0.7–2.0	
Hong Kong	0.7–1.5		
Singapore	0.8–1.8		
Sydney		1.0–2.5; typical 1.5	
Melbourne		0.6–1.5	New tram lines 0.4–0.9
Brisbane		1.0–2.0; typical 1.5	Busway 2.0–2.5
San Francisco	BART CBD 0.7–0.9; inner 1.4–1.7; outer 2.3–2.6	Caltrain 1.9–2.7	Tram CBD 0.5–0.7; inner 0.15–0.5
New York	0.4–0.65	Long Island 1.0–1.5	
Washington, DC	Inner 0.5–0.8; outer 1.0–1.5		
São Paulo	Inner 0.7–0.8; outer up to 1.2	1.2–5.0; typical 2.0–3.0	

but form an express service overlaying existing Metro and suburban rail networks.)

For the purpose of our theoretical model, we will examine the implications of the spacings as illustrated by Figure 6.5.

800 m station spacing

The catchment areas for a typical walking distance of 400 m (Figure 6.5(a)) will touch while the 800 m maximum walking distance catchments will

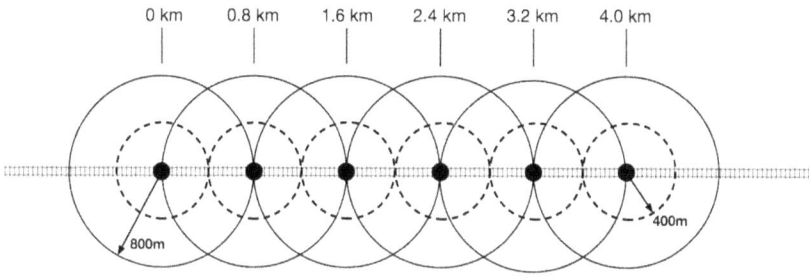

(a)

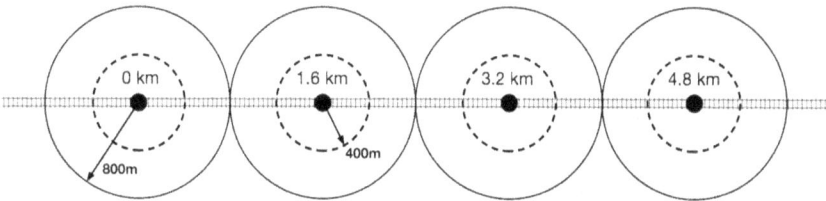

(b)

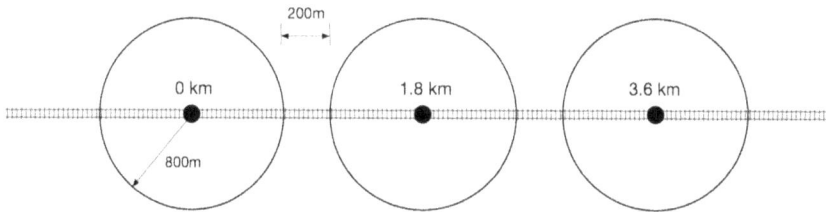

(c)

Figure 6.5 Alternative distances for ped-shed spacing

Source: Diagram © Tony Hall.

overlap. This station spacing represents the upper limit of typical city centre or dense urban metro systems. The effect in a *beads-on-string* urban form equates to a continuous linear urban form or *linear city*.

1600 m station spacing

In Figure 6.5 (b) there is no overlap of maximum walking distance catchments and the station spacing approximates to the upper limit for suburban rail services.

1800 m station spacing

While still in the region of the upper limit for suburban rail services, the 200 m gap (Figure 6.5(c)) between the ped-sheds would allow for a 40 m wide motorway reservation and still provide open green areas to separate the ped-sheds. This would allow a motorway to cross the line of the *string* without passing through a built-up area. It would also allow space for a park-and-ride facility with a 50 m wide station and a 100 m wide station car park. Where this occurred, the station spacing would be 900 m but not all the 200 m gaps would necessarily contain these facilities. However, a more comprehensive approach would be for them to be located with non-residential ped-sheds, as discussed above and illustrated by Figure 6.4.

Dealing with residential density

What will be the number of people living in the ped-shed? As noted above, some may be non-residential and some may be predominantly retail or commercial with a component of residential land use. However, most can be expected to be predominantly residential with a comparatively small area of mixed uses around the public transport station. As discussed in Chapter 3, the threshold of population needed to support specific facilities is a perennially difficult one because it is subject to change over time. For example, variations in the economics of retailing affect the support for different types of shops. The catchment areas of schools may be affected by changing educational theories and economics. Moreover, there can be different threshold populations for different types of facility. The solution proposed here is that the *area* is fixed and it is *density* that should vary according to the number of people required to support a facility. This contrasts with the more usual approach of density being regarded as fixed and uniform and the number of people required for the catchment area generating the area of the settlement. The *beads-on-string* form provides a physical framework within which the variation takes place.

Different densities in different *beads* (i.e. ped-sheds) would support a different mixture of facilities. The variation would not just be between ped-sheds but could change over time through the process of redevelopment. The point to note is that any disequilibrium within a ped-shed can be compensated for by easy travel to another nearby or to a city centre. The 800 m maximum radius would be inviolate but the intensity could change over time. Density would depend on:

* catchment area of facilities;
* response to different family types;
* economic pressures;
* distance to major centres;
* response to different characteristics of physical locations, for example lower densities where there is an interface with the countryside.

A limiting factor on residential density at the lower end of the spectrum would be the minimum catchment area of primary schools. It is advantageous for the health of children for them to be able to walk to school and the design of urban areas should not rule this out. This would imply a sufficient number of families living within a maximum radius of, say, 400 m to support such a school. The physical design of such a school would be fairly robust and should be capable of expansion. However, when laying out a new settlement, a new facility would be built as would dwellings surrounding it and at an initial density. As has been stressed, the size and composition of the population may vary in the short term and density of dwellings may change, normally increase, in the long term.

Density has two components: the physical structure which would be a medium-term variable, and people living and working in this physical form which would be a shorter-term consideration. Density would be expressed though the measure of the number of dwellings, rather than persons, per hectare (dph). Different ped-sheds would have varying designs in terms of the mixture and distribution of dwelling types. This would provide a physical, as opposed to land use, framework for the planning process. It can be argued that this is essential for sustainable planning (Hall, 2000) and this argument will be pursued further in Chapter 9. The number of people living in the dwellings would not be a specified number but would be a responsive variable, responding, in particular, to distance from major centres. It is suggested that this would be a more realistic basis for physical planning.

Approximate quantitative estimates for the physical density can be made via a rule of thumb calculation if assumptions are made about the values assigned to the variables involved. Such assumptions serve to emphasise the variability in these quantities over space and time and the need, therefore, to have physical frameworks within which these variations can be contained. The total area of the ped-shed is known from simple geometry. The non-residential areas, such as that taken up by the railway station, can be deducted from it. An initial factor for gross residential density can then be applied to the remaining area, giving a first estimate of the number of dwellings. This figure can then be multiplied by a standard for local public open space expressed as square metres per dwelling. The resulting quantity for aggregate open space can then be deducted from the residential area and calculation of residential density repeated. Assumptions relating to block dimensions and desired net-density could also be introduced into the calculation at this point.

Back of envelope calculations on this basis by the author show that, at a density of 30-35 dph, an 800 m ped-shed could contain 5000 dwellings. This assumes a local open space standard consistent with the venerable British publication *The Six Acre Standard* (NPFA, 1992). By marginally varying the assumptions, this estimate could range from 3500 to 6000 dwellings. To proceed to estimates of a resident population for the 800 m ped-shed requires the assumption of a dwelling occupancy. This again is a quantity that can be expected to change over long time periods. A rule of thumb estimate for the 800 m residential ped-shed may give a range of population from 5000 to 10,000 persons. The very imprecision of such estimates supports the argument of this book. To start from population and then hope to end up with a physical outcome on that basis would seem risky and imprecise. To start with a physical frame and then to manage variation in residential density as it occurs would appear more sensible.

Would the ped-sheds be neighbourhoods?

It is suggested that this approach might help to resolve some of the issues associated with the *neighbourhood unit* as proposed during the first half of the twentieth century. The idea of creating new neighbourhoods, more specifically *neighbourhood units*, as a principle of good town planning has had a long history and the story has been told by many authors. (Readers may find the overview provided by David Walters (2007) particularly useful.) At times, the idea has generated much controversy. To try to understand why, it may be helpful to distinguish between different aspects of a planned neighbourhood. There is the purely functional aspect, already discussed in this book, of minimum catchment populations for retail, social, educational and health facilities in order to make them viable. A normative slant can be applied to this by locating dwellings within walking distance so that people have the option of reaching them on foot as, indeed, is done in this book. This not only saves energy and encourages a healthy lifestyle, but also provides the opportunity for face-to-face contact, as discussed in previous chapters. Contemporary urban design principles stress this as necessary for personal security and sociability. However, it was primarily the encouragement of strong social relations within neighbourhoods that was stressed by the progenitors of the neighbourhood principle in planning and it was this same goal, rather than the more functional considerations, that gave rise to controversy.

Walkable urban areas can be found within new planned cities from Adelaide, Australia, through to the English garden cities. However, the planned *neighbourhood unit* as such was first proposed in the USA by Clarence Perry in 1929 (Perry, 1929). It had a five-minute walk (1/4 mile, 400 m) radius around a school and civic facilities but with the shops on the edge at the intersection of main roads. It was given physical form in Clarence Stein and Henry Wright's 1928 plan for Radburn, New Jersey. However, his proposal was not subsequently taken up and applied by residential developers as a general principle in the USA or any other country. Its realisation had to await the advent of totally planned towns. It was given its most complete, critics would say most rigid, expression in the British Mark 1 New Towns of the 1950s. Outside their town centres, the entire town was composed of neighbourhoods that were physically separate from each other (i.e. they did not overlap) and which were focused on a primary school and local shops. Local shops were not permitted outside the neighbourhood centres. Whatever view is taken of the rigidity of this policy, the motives behind it were benign and the intention was to create clear and strong local identities both for each residential neighbourhood and the town as a whole, all of which had clearly defined spatial boundaries.

It was this pure-line approach, as adopted in the British Mark 1 New Towns and elsewhere, that provoked some trenchant criticism during the late 1960s. One was from Christopher Alexander (1966) in his short piece, 'The City is Not a Tree'. He argued that people's social relations did not conform to a hierarchy of nested urban forms with connections like the branches of a tree. He preferred the concept of the *semi-lattice* with relationships being permitted to occur across all spatial boundaries and levels in a spatial hierarchy. In the same year, Maurice Broady launched his attack on *architectural determinism* (Broady, 1966) by which he meant attempts to create the bonds of community through the physical design of new urban form and to design it on the basis that this would always happen. However, Broady did concede, as many other authors have also conceded, that physical form can influence behaviour even if it cannot determine it. Further criticism came in the 1960s from Melvin Webber (Webber, 1964) arguing that the car-borne *non-place urban realm* that had emerged in the form of the car-based American suburb and *edge city* had rendered the whole notion of sociability through physical proximity obsolete. However, whereas the theorists saw a dichotomy, the situation on the ground became more complex. Where planning was weak then car-based urban form, without clear neighbourhood structures, emerged just as Webber had observed and predicted. Nevertheless, where planning was strong, physical neighbourhood structures were still present. The English *new city* of Milton Keynes, as one rather extreme example, had both physically separated neighbourhoods (with large gaps and major roads between) but within a motorway grid. There was also the matter of *perceived identity* by which people saw themselves as belonging to a neighbourhood independently, sometimes, of its physical delineation. Perceived local identity, as any estate agent will confirm, is important to people especially when they are faced with unstructured and undifferentiated suburbia. This debate did not prevent professional planning practice from proceeding and innovating, but the economic and political pressures experienced during the 1980s did, or at least attempted to, prevent further progress on the ground. It was not until the 1990s that further substantial ideas on neighbourhood planning were published.

The year 1993 saw the publication of two independent proposals for design of the *beads* on the string. Breheny and Rookwood (1993) considered the ideal patterns of development needed for a sustainable city region in Britain. Amongst proposals for the layout of existing city centres, the inner city, suburbs and mixed urban and rural areas, they made proposals for 'small towns and new communities', as illustrated by the diagram in Figure 6.6. They were to be located away from 'development corridors'.

Development was to be centred on a heavy rail station but confined within 'lines of containment'. There would be a light rail connection to other similar settlements. Internal movement was to be based a local bus loop, rather than the settlement being completely walkable. At the intersection of the heavy rail, light rail and bus routes there would be a mixed-use centre, with higher-density housing located adjacent to it. If edge-of-settlement 'superstores', presumably with surface car parking, were necessary, they would be located on the light rail line.

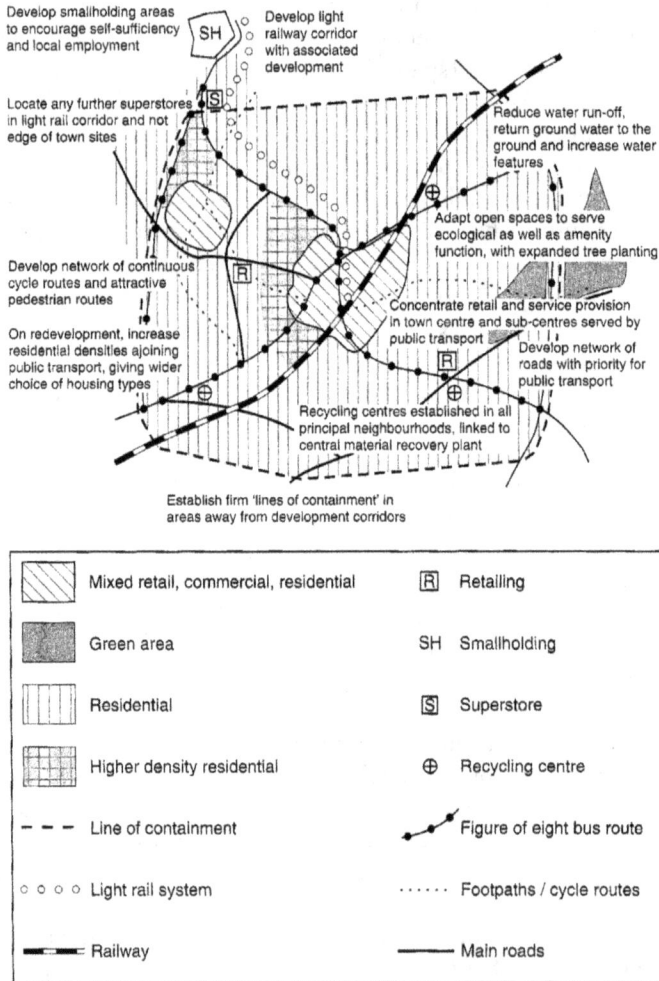

Figure 6.6 The idealised new settlement proposal made by Breheny and Rookwood in 1993

Source: Reproduced from Andrew Blowers (ed.) *Planning for a Sustainable Environment: A Report by the Town and Country Planning Association,* Earthscan, 1993, courtesy of the TCPA.

The other proposal of that year, the *transit-oriented development* (TOD) of Peter Calthorpe (1993), has become much better known. It is illustrated by Figure 6.7. All TODs would have a radius of 10 minutes walk, interpreted as a distance of 2000 ft (610 m). Calthorpe made a distinction between *urban* and *neighbourhood* TODs. *Urban* TODs were to be centred on a station on a major, normally rail-based, transit route. They would have a 'commercial core' containing shops, restaurants, local offices, entertainment and community facilities with, possibly, high-density housing situated above them. Substantial office employment and high-density housing would be located immediately adjacent to the commercial core. Housing at comparatively lower densities would surround these areas, with an average density of 15 dpa (dwellings per acre) (37 dph) and a minimum of 12 dpa (30 dph). The *neighbourhood* TODs would be located on 'feeder bus' routes within 10 minutes bus ride of a main railway station. They would have a 'commercial core' containing a minimum of a convenience store and local offices. The surrounding housing would have an average density of 10 dpa (25 dph) and a minimum of 7 dpa (17 dph). Roads within all TODs would normally be 'connected streets' (i.e. no cul-de-sacs) with vistas for way-finding where appropriate. Traffic speeds would be limited to 15 mph (24 kph) on 8 ft (2.4 m) traffic lanes. Street parking was not just to be allowed but encouraged. With parking lanes, footways and four lines of trees, the road reservations could end up quite wide. 'Connector streets' would link these streets with 'arterial' roads. These four to six lane 'arterials' would cater for through traffic although pedestrians and cyclists would cross them at the same level. For large retail and commercial premises, parking would be to the rear allowing direct active frontage to the street. Park-and-ride facilities would be physically separate from TODs.

So far, these ideas, particularly the *urban TODs*, have a general correspondence to those proposed here. There are, however, two important

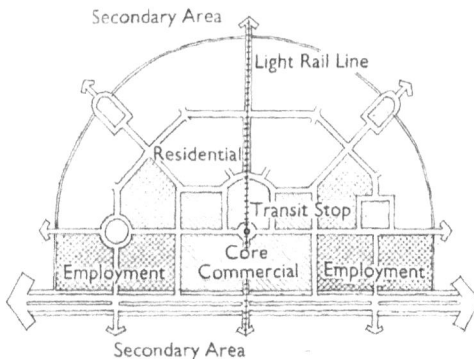

Figure 6.7 Peter Calthorpe's diagram for 'urban transit oriented development'

Source: Peter Calthorpe, *The Next American Metropolis,* 1993. Reproduced by permission of the Princeton Architectural Press

points of difference. One is that Calthorpe's TODs are semicircular. They are placed on a major road but do not cross it. For *neighbourhood TODs*, the feeder bus routes would run along the arterial roads. For *urban TODs* the railway line would lie at right angles to the arterial. For the proposals here, the arterials run within the non-built-up areas and the ped-sheds are circular. The second major difference is that Calthorpe envisaged the TODs being surrounded by 'secondary areas', stretching out to a maximum radius of one mile (1.6 km) from the transit stop at the centre of the TOD. These would contain 'single family houses' at low densities. (Calthorpe appears to mean, by this term, detached houses with space around them. Terraced or semi-detached (duplex) houses would not be 'single family houses' in his terminology.) These areas would also contain 'secondary employment', a term that would exclude those activities found within the commercial core as well warehouses and low-intensity manufacturing. This leaves, by implication, compact light industry in the 'secondary areas'. For the proposals here, development is limited to ped-sheds which are thus surrounded by *green* non-built-up areas. Low-intensity, non-residential uses would have their own ped-sheds.

In the general American debates of 1990s in more progressive circles, the pendulum swung back to neighbourhoods in the context of American New Urbanism, which has already been discussed in Chapter 5. This incorporated both Calthorpe's TODs and Duany Plater-Zyberk's *traditional neighbourhood development* (DPZ, 2002). Its proportions were very similar to those of Clarence Perry's original with the same 1/4 mile radius. This idea became one of the founding principles of New Urbanism. The problem, though, with most aspects of New Urbanism, has been one of implementation. When and where has it actually been implemented and, where examples do occur, are they good ones? Certainly, in the USA and also Australia, New Urbanism has not been the general policy and New Urbanist settlements are not widespread on the ground. The notable exception has been Western Australia's *Liveable Neighbourhoods* policy (WAPC, 2004). Here, the 400 m radius around local shops became a key element of the policy. However, it is not a planning requirement for local education and health facilities. Here we come to a real and practical planning problem. Where planning systems merely control private house building, how can they ensure that neighbourhood facilities for education and health will be provided by other departments of government? The creation of real neighbourhoods requires comprehensive planning powers on a 'new town' scale and it has been in new towns that they have been most in evidence.

Returning to the theory, as opposed to the very important issue of implementation, we can examine the neighbourhood question by putting it in its negative form of why should new urban form not have walkable neighbourhoods? Is there any pressing reason why they should not be the norm? If we were to ask the contemporary suburban residents, one answer they might give is that they do not want to be sociable. Electronic communication is safer. Getting away from others is a useful solution to problems. As Sartre put it, 'hell is other people'. However, to go much further in this direction would take the argument outside the scope of this book. As popular as such sentiments may be in reality, they are not consistent with the values of the planned city. A more practical reason for not providing walkable neighbourhoods, irrespective of whether people want to be sociable or not, is the desire for full motorisation – the ability to use a car at all times and to go to all places. Although popular and advantageous, the ability to fulfil this dream was disposed of in Chapter 2 on the basis that, in the final analysis, it is not physically possible. A walkable neighbourhood with car access, but not designed around the car, offers the possibility of face-to-face social connections rather than ruling them out.

The approach proposed here should provide a physical basis for local identity, while achieving a flexible response to the changing nature of commercial and service provision, through linking areas with a variety of densities and local functions. The smallest ped-shed would still contain a primary school and some local shops, thus bearing a clear similarity to the neighbourhood unit but without its rigidity or social assumptions.

Summary

A general method for designing sustainable settlements has begun to emerge from the theoretical considerations presented in Chapters 2 and 3. New towns and cities, and their extensions, would be made up of strings of predominantly residential ped-sheds of varying density and function. They would share the following properties.

- At their centre a public transport node on a quality public transport corridor, ideally a track-based facility.
- This node would be surrounded by a mixture of residential, commercial and community uses, overlapping in three dimensions, or on immediately adjacent plots all within a radius of, say, around 100 m.
- This local centre would be surrounded by primarily residential and educational uses at comparatively lower density within walking distance, say an 800 m radius.
- All residential ped-sheds would contain a minimum level of provision of shops, schools and leisure opportunities. Higher-density ped-sheds would contain a wider range of facilities. The population as a whole would be able to access the complete range via the transport corridor.
- The ped-shed would be surrounded by open green areas containing recreational and agricultural activities. These could be extended into green wedges between strings of ped-sheds.
- In addition to the predominantly residential ped-sheds, there could be others that were predominantly non-residential containing park-and-ride facilities and low-intensity commercial, health and educational facilities.

What the *beads-on-string* form provides is a physical solution that is robust over space and time. It is the physical structure that is designed, has permanence and delivers sustainability. The nature and intensity of land uses would change over time within the physical structure. As the threshold population for the support of different facilities changes over time and space so the intensity of use can respond.

References

Alexander, Christopher (1966) The City is Not a Tree, *Design*, 206, 46–55.

Breheny, Michael and Rookwood, Ralph (1993) Planning the Sustainable City Region, in *Planning for a Sustainable Environment: A Report by the Town and Country Planning Association*, edited by Andrew Blowers, London: Earthscan, pp. 150–189.

Broady, Maurice (1966) Social Theory in Architectural Design, *Arena: The Architectural Association Journal*, 81, pp. 149–154.

Calthorpe, Peter (1993) *The Next American Metropolis: Ecology, Community and the American Dream*, New York: Princeton Architectural Press.

DPZ, Duany Plater-Zyberk & Co (2002) *The Lexicon of New Urbanism, Version 3.2*, Miami, FL: DPZ.

Hall, A. C. (2000) A New Paradigm for Development Plans, *Urban Design International*, 5(2), pp. 123–140.

Llewelyn Davies, English Partnerships and the Housing Corporation (2000) *Urban Design Compendium Volume 1*, London: English Partnerships and the Housing Corporation.

NPFA, National Playing Fields Association (1992) *The Six Acre Standard: Minimum Standards for Outdoor Playing Space*, London: National Playing Fields Association.

Perry, Clarence (1929) *The Neighborhood Unit: A Scheme of Arrangement for the Family-Life Community*, Regional Study of New York and Its Environs VII, Neighborhood and Community Planning, Monograph One, 2-140, New York: Regional Plan of New York and Its Environs.

Viljoen, André and Bohn, Katrin (eds) (2014) *Second Nature Urban Agriculture: Designing Productive Cities*, Abingdon: Routledge.

Walker, Jarrett (2012) *Human Transit: How Clearer Thinking about Public Transit Can Enrich Our Communities and Our Lives*, Portland, OR: Island Press.

Walters, David (2007) *Designing Community: Charrettes, Master Plans and Form-based Codes*, Amsterdam and London: Elsevier/Architectural Press.

Webber, Melvin (1964) The Urban Place and the Nonplace Urban Realm, in *Explorations into Urban Structure*, edited by M. M. Webber, Philadelphia, PA: University of Pennsylvania Press, pp. 79–163.

White, Peter (2009) *Public Transport: Its Planning, Management and Operation*, 5th ed., London: Routledge.

WAPC, Western Australian Planning Commission (2004) *Liveable Neighbourhoods Edition 3*, Perth: Government of Western Australia.

7 A model for a new city

The purpose of this chapter is to take the *beads-on-string* form developed in Chapter 6 and to arrange the *strings* into a whole city model. This will be an idealised form, not an actual city plan, that will extend the theoretical model so that its properties citywide can be examined. It will be shown that the goals of sustainability and quality of life can lead to a uniquely robust pattern of city form and that this pattern has remarkable, even novel, qualities.

Lattice or radial structures?

There are two basic alternatives for the way the *beads on a string* could be put together, lattice or radial structures. There are in turn a number of variants on these and they are illustrated by Figure 7.1. The strings could be arranged in a lattice in a compact form, as shown by Figure 7.1(a), with each ped-shed being served by two public transport lines, or dispersed, with only a limited number of ped-sheds being so connected, as shown by Figure 7.1(b). The roads for motor vehicles would run in the spaces between the ped-sheds forming an equivalent grid. Such lattices could be *non-directional*, free to expand in any direction, or *directional*, constrained to a bias along one particular line. The alternative arrangement is a radial structure, as shown by Figure 7.1(c), where both public transport lines and roads originate from a unique centre. Separate radial *cities* can be linked via a *hub-and-spoke* structure, as shown by Figure 7.1(d). The difference between the lattice and radial approaches hinges on the identification of *centres* of activity. In the radial structure, they are predefined and there is a clear hierarchy. For the lattice structure, although centres are not precluded they may arise *naturally* over time. The significant point is that the centres are not predetermined.

To make our choice, it is possible to consider real examples rather than rely on further theoretical considerations. Throughout history, cities have tended to expand radially along lines of movement from centres of activity. It is true that in many parts of the world, a particular example would be North America, new development since the late eighteenth century has been guided by rectangular grids for street layout. It is also true that planned settlements across the world since ancient times have used very formal grid

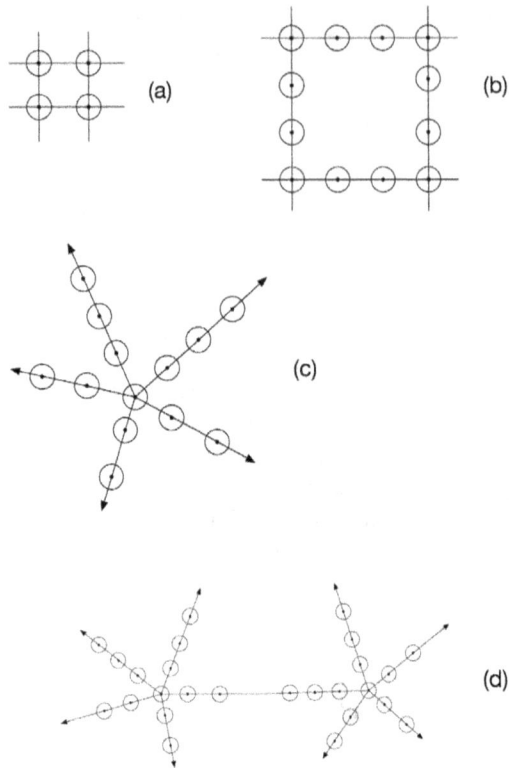

Figure 7.1 Alternative ways of combining 'beads-on-string' form

Source: Diagram © Tony Hall

layouts for streets. However, this is not what we are talking about here, but rather how large cities grew. Did they develop a major city centre, with a subsequent hierarchy of subsidiary centres and did development spread out from these centres in an approximately radial direction? Looking at the growth of major cities across the world, although the nature and intensity of urban activities may change over time, the pattern and hierarchy of urban centres can be surprisingly constant.

It is also a valid point that, in some parts of the world, clearly defined, free-standing cities cannot be easily discerned. In the western parts of North America and Australia, cities can have a clear spatial separation with expanses of terrain containing few major settlements between them. On the other hand, in Western Europe and the Northeast USA, urban areas merge together to form a *megalopolis* with no clear boundaries. The suburban centres within Greater London would be major cities in their own right if they could be separated out. The Ruhr in Germany and the Randstad in the Netherlands could be seen as urban agglomerations transcending the city administrations of which they are composed. However, in all these circumstances a clear hierarchy of centres is still discernible, as is a radial pattern of movement on a hub-and-spoke pattern within their component cities. In contrast, lattice structures without clearly defined and concentrated centres are much rarer and are almost always car-based. The nearest approximations to a non-directional grid may be found in suburban Los Angeles, California, for example in the San Fernando Valley, and Ontario. For examples of directional grids, there is the suburban development stretching along US 95 in southern Florida. None of these examples offers any degree of sustainability nor are they planned settlements, which is the subject of discussion here.

In the late 1960s, several new cities were proposed for Southeast England (SEEPC, 1967) and the fashion of the time was the car-based, non-directional grid as epitomised by the plan for South Hampshire (Colin Buchanan and Partners, 1966), a city that was never ultimately built. This planning principle was infused by thinking epitomised by the views of the American academic, Melvin Webber (Webber, 1964), whose phrase *the non-place urban realm* became a byword. The argument was that the car-based suburban form of southern California was an inevitable consequence of the equally inevitable growth of car use. This represented the future and it should be planned for accordingly. There was, indeed, a lot to be said for this inevitability. The popularity of private and commercial motor vehicles could not be denied. The subsequent spread of the car-based urban form over North America and then to other parts of the world, in the absence of planning controls to prevent it, it was a stark phenomenon. The repetitive design and lack of sense of place exhibited by car-based shopping centres and office parks was equally stark, but was perceived by many as evidence of progress. It was happening then and has continued to happen. In the context of the planning of new cities in late 1960s Britain, this argument also had traction. A grid of motor roads would establish a planning principle for the layout of urban form without the need for a rigid master plan. (Indeed, the idea that physical planning can be based on principles rather than rigid, long-term layouts will be argued in this very book.) Such grids, although usable by local buses, would not be very good for facilitating the provision of quality public transport. However, in many quarters at that time public transport was seen as old-fashioned and loss-making, not the stuff of a visionary future. The ultimate weakness of the argument was the impossibility of designing a road system that could physically accommodate all the desired cars, as argued in Chapter 2, and the lack of concern for sustainability in all its forms which was not a goal in that time period.

Although the South Hampshire city was never built, there was, however, one example of the construction of a totally new city planned on the basis of a compact non-directional grid and that was Milton Keynes in England, already referred to in a previous chapter (MKDC, 2014). Milton Keynes was the only one of its type to be built. Its plan was based on a 1 km grid of roads. They were built as motor roads with limited frontage to, and access from, other land uses. Within the kilometre-grid cells were housing areas that were somewhat smaller in size than the ped-sheds proposed here and usually had medium-density terraced housing and contained local schools. However, they did not have pre-planned identifiable mixed-use cores with local shops, small-scale employment and community facilities situated adjacent to each other. A completely segregated network of footpath–cycleways was also built. The original idea was that local facilities might grow up naturally around the intersections of this grid with the motor road grid but this never happened. The tendency was to locate some shops and other facilities in the centre of housing estates within each grid square. Two observations need to be made in relation to the argument being discussed here. Firstly, the housing areas proved difficult to serve efficiently and effectively by public transport as the buses needed to turn off the main roads of the grid and pass slowly through the housing areas in a circuitous fashion. Secondly, in practice the grid was not really non-directional. There was no *naturally evolving* pattern of centres but, instead, one, planned, principal city centre, served eventually by an intercity railway service, within which all major shopping and entertainment facilities were focused. Milton Keynes does, therefore, have a major centre which is commercially successful and no one has ever argued that it should be replaced, or competed with, by facilities dispersed across the grid.

No further planned cities of this type have been constructed and, therefore, there is no additional evidence of the consequences of a planned non-directional grid. There does not appear to be any hard evidence from any source that a lattice would have an advantage over a radial structure if goals of sustainability were being pursued. On the other hand, the requirement for an effective and high-quality public transport system, ideally track-based, would imply a radial structure linked to other cities via a hub-and-spoke structure.

Construction of the city model

For the theoretical city model to be considered here, a radial structure will be adopted. The *beads-on-string* can be arranged in such a pattern, with *arms* or *fingers* radiating out from a central point. Towards the end of Chapter 6, the implications of different spacings of the ped-sheds were discussed. These different spacings, together with different angular separations of the radial *arms*, can now be used to generate alternative radial patterns of city form from which the functional implications of each alternative can be assessed. This is not, in itself, novel and similar suggestions by other authors are discussed, for purposes of comparison, later in this chapter. The innovation proposed, and pursued, here will be to insert additional radial 'arms' between others where space allows, with these arms being served by branches from the public transport lines.

We will start with a line of 800 m ped-sheds overlapping by 800 m, the maximum walking distance. This will provide public transport stops every 800 m, as discussed in Chapter 6 and illustrated by Figure 6.5. If the ped-

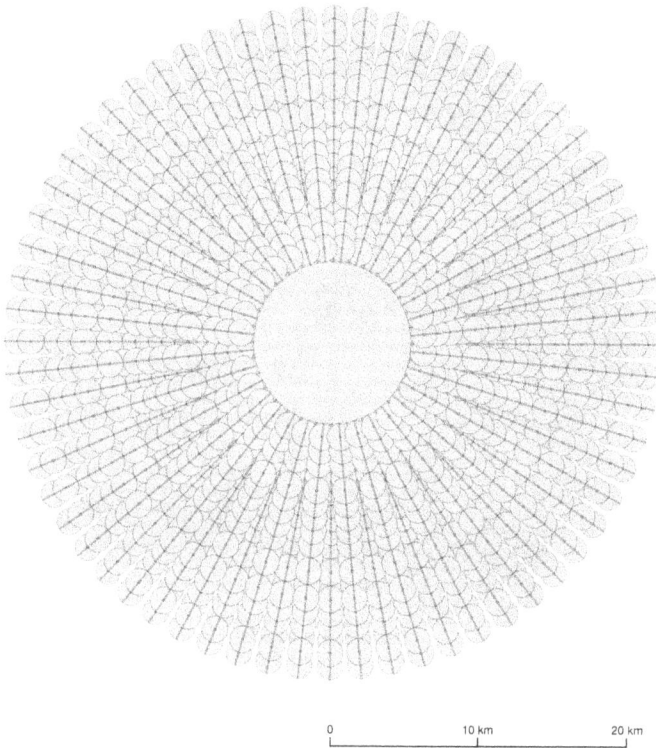

Figure 7.2 800 m radius ped-sheds overlapping linearly and radially; station stops every 400 m

Source: Diagram © Tony Hall.

sheds overlap on radial separation, as well as linearly, then the form shown in Figure 7.2 results. It produces, in effect, a continuous built-up area. It does not produce open spaces adjacent to the ped-sheds that could accommodate large-scale recreational provision and motorways. In addition, all major roads have to pass through built-up areas. Although it has a very high density of public transport lines and stops, it does not otherwise represent a significant departure from an existing planned city. There is no scope for the easy and cheap retrofitting of infrastructure.

The next step is to introduce a minimum separation of at least 200 m between the radial forms. The result is shown by Figure 7.3. Note the use of the *branching* public transport routes and the pattern of urban form that they generate. This produces *non-built-up areas* between the radiating linear forms, except for the *city centre* where there is a continuous built-up area with a radius of at least 1 km. There is now space for large-scale recreational facilities, radial motorways and for the construction of express public transport lines bypassing the ped-sheds. By changing trains (if necessary)

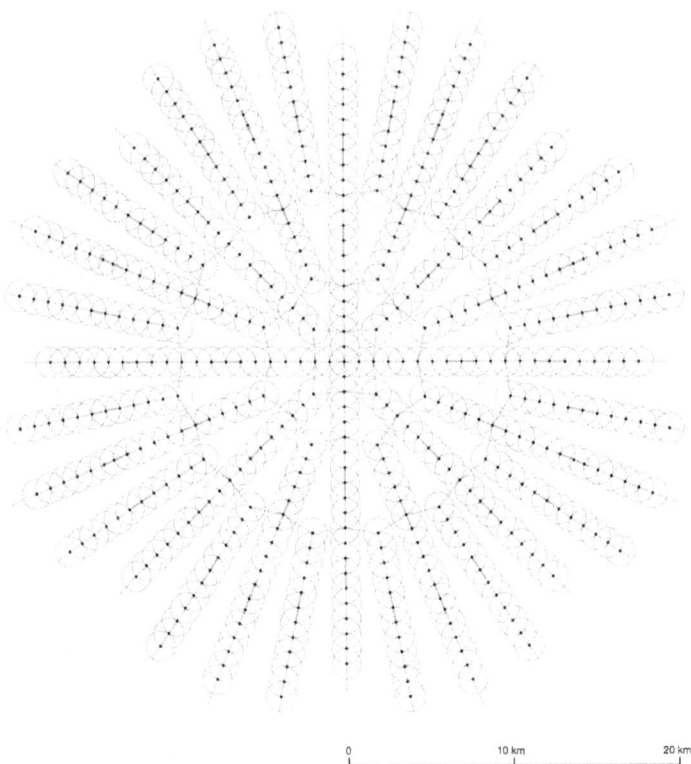

Figure 7.3 800 m radius ped-sheds overlapping linearly by 800 m and with a minimum 200 m of radial separation; station stops every 400 m

Source: Diagram © Tony Hall.

it would be possible to make circular trips by public transport around the city. However, with stops every 400 m for journeys of at least 10 km, most of the public transport trips would not be very rapid. The most significant disadvantage is that circular motorways within the city could not be provided without passing through the built-up areas.

We can now turn to the consideration of the conclusion of the argument in Chapter 6, that the use of 800 m ped-sheds with a separation of 200 m offers the most advantages. Major roads can pass between them permitting circular routes around and throughout the city. There is green space within walking distance of all residents. The 200 m gap also permits park-and-ride stations between the ped-sheds, where a major road crosses the public transport line, although non-residential ped-sheds may provide a more comprehensive solution for park-and-ride facilities. Figure 7.4(a) shows a city model on this basis extending to a maximum radius of approximately 10 km. Note the emergence of circular or orbital public transport routes at 3.6 km and 9 km radii from the city centre.

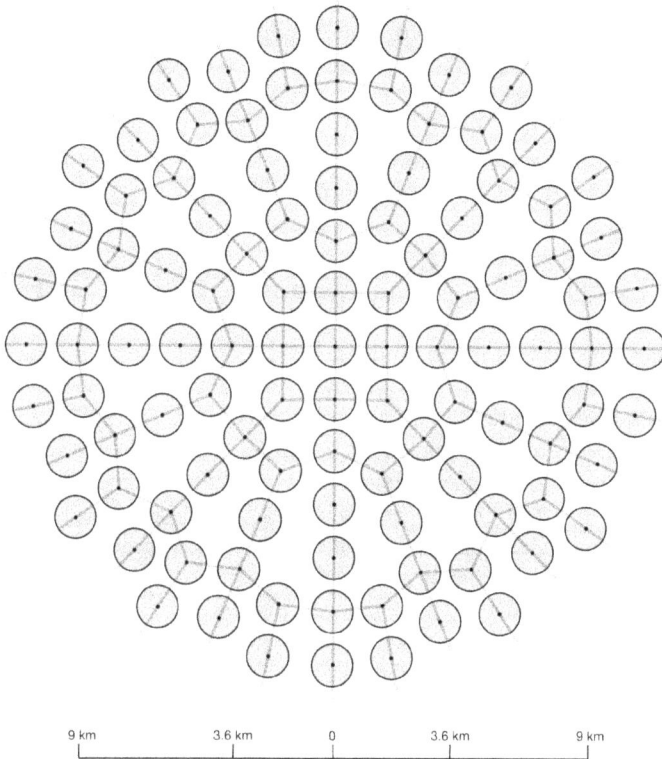

Figure 7.4(a) 800 m radius ped-sheds with 200 m separation; station stops every 1800 m; city radius approximately 10 km

Source: Diagram © Tony Hall.

One property of this city model needs special emphasis. Outside the city centre, substantial non-built-up areas between the *beads-on-string* are created. As the extent of the city grows so these areas become largely enclosed on all sides with only narrow connecting strips between them. As such, they are not really *green wedges* in conventional planning parlance, as these normally remain open-ended as the city grows. The term that will be used here for the non-built-up areas will be *green enclaves*. Starting 4 km out from the centre, each one is approximately 5.5 km long and varies in width from 0.5 km to over 2 km, with a total area of approximately 560 ha. These are areas that can accommodate a wide range of uses (other than continuous built-up areas). They could accommodate roads for motor traffic and railway lines for high-speed passenger and heavy freight movements, in addition to the recreational facilities and urban agriculture whose merits have been discussed in Chapter 6.

At first glance, the diagram may appear very uniform, as though all the ped-sheds would be the same, but this would not necessarily be the case.

What is being presented is a long-term physical structure. As discussed in Chapter 6, residential density could vary over the city, as could the quantity and scale of non-residential uses. Many of the ped-sheds could be at a much higher residential density than adjacent ones and could incorporate significant local centres. Furthermore, a number of the ped-sheds would not be predominantly residential but might have all, or a major part of, their area devoted to manufacturing or distribution activities, or to large-scale health or educational provision or to park-and-ride facilities. These variations would not only occur spatially but temporally, that is, changes would occur during the very long-term periods over which the physical structure of the city would last.

What of the city centre in Figure 7.4(a)? It is not a continuous built-up area, as in most cities. However, the central ped-shed could reach very high densities and contain a very wide range of uses, as could the ped-sheds adjacent to it. The central ped-sheds could be brought closer together than the outer ones but, whether they are or not, the prospect is of a larger central area composed of higher-density urban neighbourhoods, or *quarters*, separated by parkland while still constituting an integrated whole. Note also that an intercity railway line passing through the city could be accommodated within the green enclaves, with a main station within the central ped-shed.

The reader may now wish to know the likely population of this theoretical city. The answer is, firstly, that this is not a fixed quantity. As the residential density in terms of dwellings will vary so will the population, both for this reason and because of variation in dwelling occupancy. The whole idea is that the city is designed on the basis of the efficiency of its physical frame and infrastructure rather than for a target occupancy. Nevertheless, the calculations performed in Chapter 6 provide a guideline, albeit a rather wide one. For each residential ped-shed, the population could vary between 5000 and 10,000 persons. However, many ped-sheds would be only partially residential and some not residential at all. There are 104 ped-sheds in the diagram in Figure 7.4(a) and on this basis the total population could vary from half a million to one million people. Again, it must be emphasised that the whole idea is that a *robust* structure should accommodate a large variation in population while retaining its planned qualities.

Figure 7.4(b) shows the same theoretical city with the addition of the roads for motor vehicles where they are outside the ped-sheds. Following the argument of previous chapters, there would be a two-level road hierarchy: slow speed with active frontage and higher speed with restricted frontage. Within ped-sheds the former would apply; between the ped-sheds, the latter. We are immediately presented with a most remarkable result. It is possible to drive over the entire city at a reasonable speed on roads designed for the motor vehicle even though the city has been laid out to facilitate walking and use of public transport. A possible objection that readers may now raise, though, is that these roads are severing the green enclaves and creating barriers to the movement of their users. One immediate response

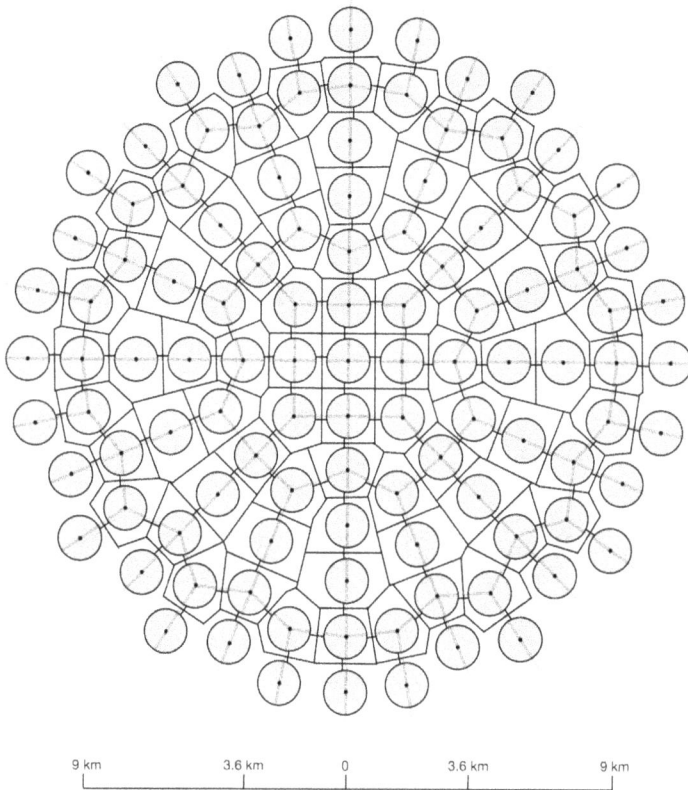

| 9 km | 3.6 km | 0 | 3.6 km | 9 km |

Figure 7.4(b) As Figure 7.4(a), but the network of restricted-frontage motor roads is now shown

Source: Diagram © Tony Hall

is that this is certainly going to be no worse that the situation in existing cities. However, there is the more important point that, although these roads may be subject to access restrictions, not all of them will be the same. Some may, indeed, be motorways with several lanes in each direction. On the other hand, and at the other extreme, many may have just one lane in each direction carrying mainly local traffic. This will, as with the population density, vary both within the city and over time. In large parts of the city, especially at the extremities, the severance will be very minor. Moreover, the large size of the green enclaves must be taken into account. They are not types of local park but areas up to 2 km wide.

Another important property of the theoretical model is that it is extendable while retaining access to public transport and green space. There is no fixed outer boundary. The land that cannot be built on is within the city rather than around it. Figure 7.5(a) shows the city expanded to a radius of approximately 20 km. The motor roads are not shown for the moment

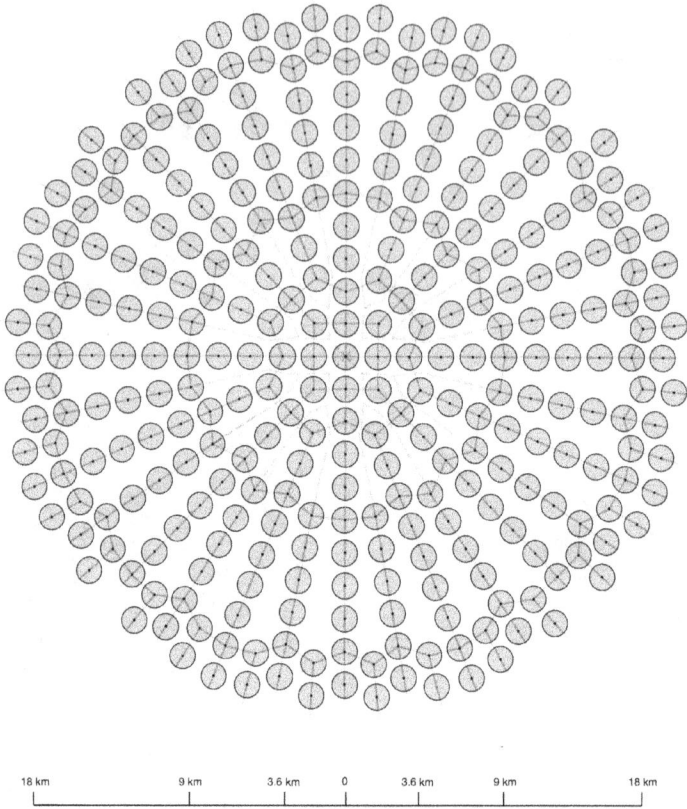

Figure 7.5(a) 800 m radius ped-sheds with 200 m separation; station stops every 1800 m; city radius approximately 20 km

Source: Diagram © Tony Hall

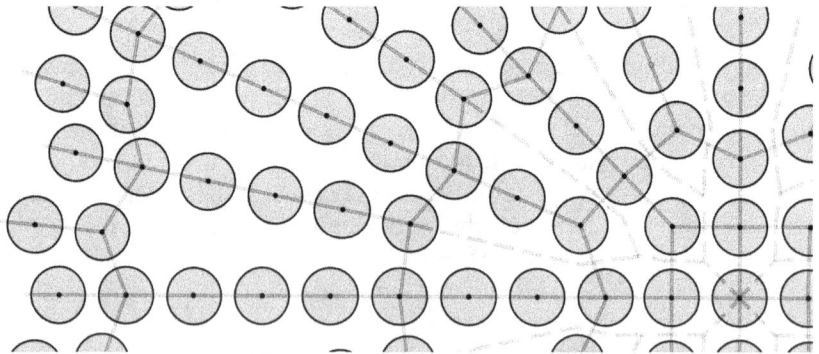

Figure 7.5(b) An enlargement of part of the city showing the possible retrofitting of express rail links within the 'green enclaves'

Source: Diagram © Tony Hall

to aid clarity. Figure 7.5 (b) shows an enlargement for part of the city. We now have another set of green enclaves. These larger enclaves, starting 9 km out from the centre, are approximately 10 km long and also vary in width from 0.5 km to over 2 km, each having a total area of approximately 1800 ha. What can now be seen is how the inner ring of green enclaves can accommodate express rail lines providing faster services from the city centre and the outer areas and retrofitted as the city expands. There is now another orbital public transport route at a radius of 18 km from the centre. There is an apparent concentration of ped-sheds at this radius but it should be noted that, were the city to expand further, there would be further green enclaves beyond. Moreover, each and all of the ped-sheds in this ring have at least 200 m of green space around them.

Figure 7.6(a) shows the model city with the motor roads (but not the express rail lines for clarity). Figure 7.6(b) shows an enlargement for part of the city. Again, all parts of the city are accessible by motor vehicles at reasonable speeds. The roads running through the inner ring of ped-sheds can be widened as the city expands. Similarly, the inner ring of ped-sheds can increase in density and accommodate larger-scale central facilities. Estimating the overall population of city on the same basis as the 10 km model gives a range of one and a half to two million inhabitants, possibly more.

Implications of the city model

Taking stock of the theoretical city model illustrated by Figures 7.5 and 7.6, it can be seen to have some remarkable properties. There is no barrier to all residents who are able to walk being able to:

- walk to a public transport stop and then travel all over the city by quality public transport and then walk to their destination;
- walk not just to local parks but also to large area of open land that can contain playing fields and other large-scale recreational facilities;
- walk to a local centre for shopping and community facilities, and access others via a public transport line;
- drive everywhere in the city on motorways, except for a slow speed section at the beginning and end of every trip which need not exceed 800 m in length;
- drive to park-and-ride facilities on the public transport lines;
- access hospitals and other major community facilities, such as stadia, by both car and public transport line.

All this can be supplemented by the provision of local bus services.

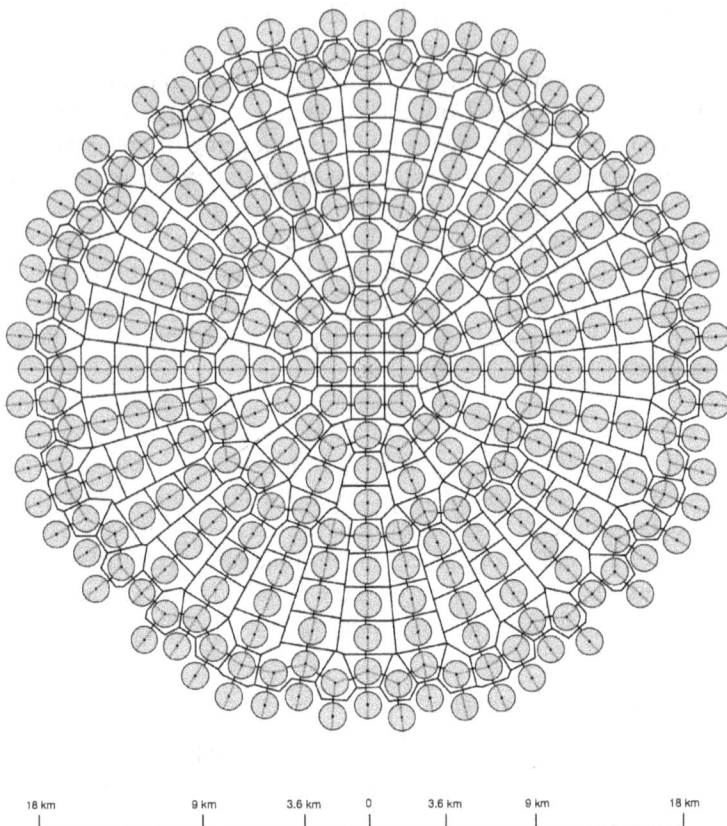

18 km   9 km   3.6 km   0   3.6 km   9 km   18 km

Figure 7.6(a) As Figure 7.5(a), but the network of restricted-frontage motor roads is now shown

Source: Diagram © Tony Hall

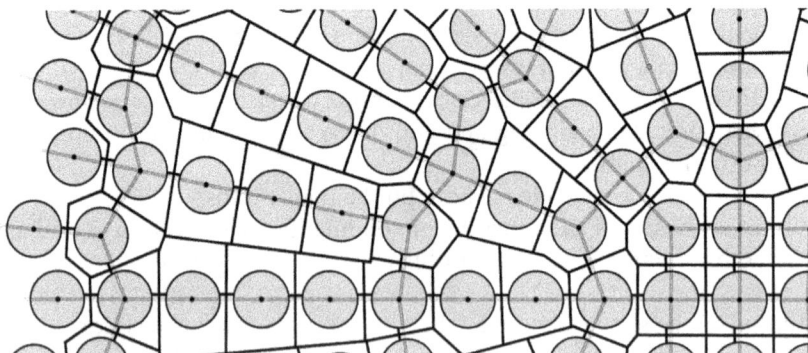

Figure 7.6(b) An enlargement of part of the city showing the network of restricted-frontage motor roads

Source: Diagram © Tony Hall

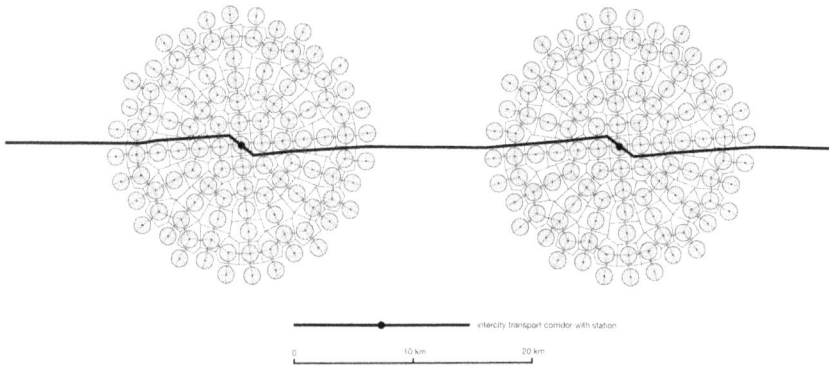

Figure 7.7 A possible linking of two 10 km radius cities

Source: Diagram © Tony Hall

City expansion and networks of cities

An important property of the theoretical city model is that it appears to be able to expand indefinitely while retaining its sustainable characteristics. The city model also allows for retrofitting of infrastructure as it expands. *Indefinitely* is, of course, a theoretical concept here. In reality, the city would encounter other settlements as it expands and would eventually meet other large cities. However, this can also be incorporated within the theoretical model. Additional *radial cities* on the lines described here could be place adjacent to, and integrated with, each other on a hub-and-spoke basis, as was illustrated by Figure 7.1(d).

Figure 7.7 shows two 10 km radius cities linked by an intercity transport corridor containing a main-line railway and a motorway. (The motorway would not enter the central ped-shed.) Cities could be strung along the transport corridor to create a higher level of *beads-on-string* form. Notwithstanding the ability of each theoretical city model to expand sustainably in a radial direction, would indefinite expansion be a good idea in reality? Figure 7.8 shows two 20 km radius cities with their centres approximately 40 km apart. As they merge into each other a higher concentration of ped-sheds results such that another *city* could be said to emerge, but in an unplanned way. In particular, there would be no new radial public transport routes to a new *centre* unless retrofitted on a massive scale. This is not in line with the intention of designing the planned robust city.

Figure 7.9 shows 20 km radius cities with a gap of approximately 10 km between them. Additional ped-sheds are allowed along the line of the intercity route but not otherwise. Radial expansion is restricted in favour of the building or expansion of other cities. However, there is ample space around the cities to permit this not to be taken as a rigid and literal rule. The figure shows how the cities could possibly be arranged on

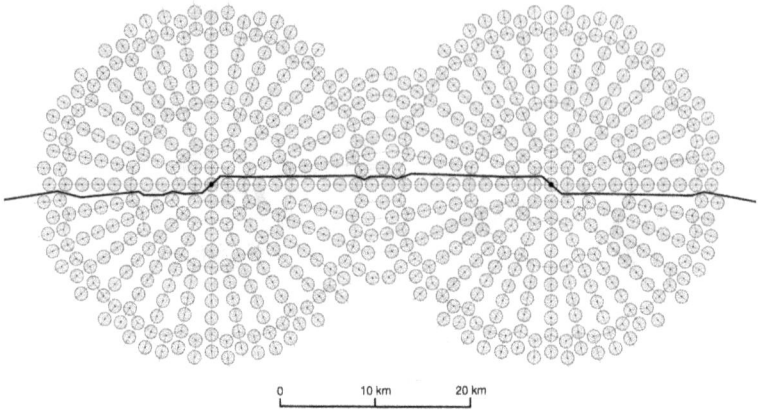

Figure 7.8 The effect of merging two 20 km radius cities

Source: Diagram © Tony Hall

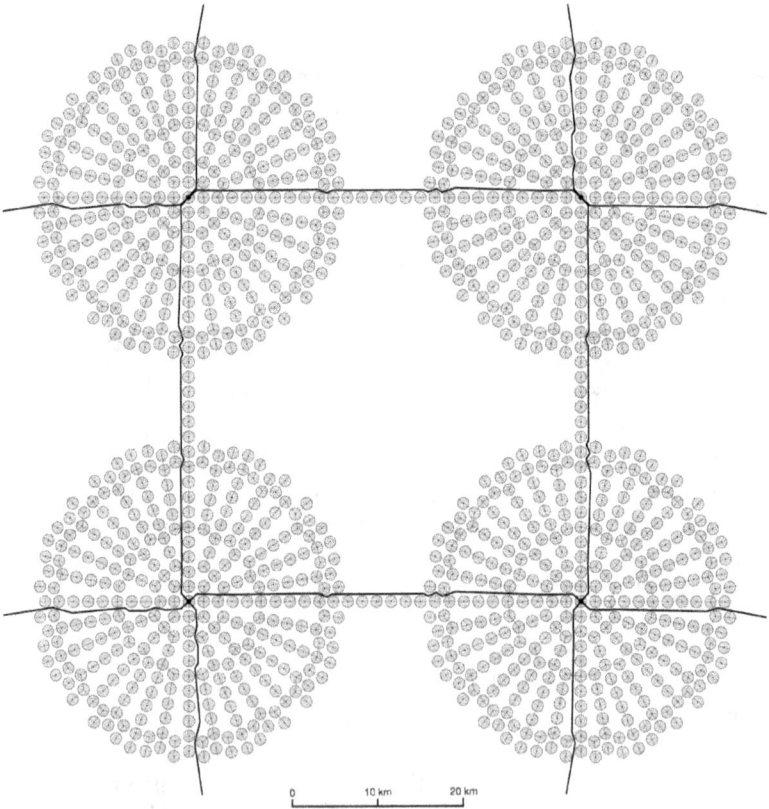

Figure 7.9 A lattice of 20 km radius cities separated by 10 km

Source: Diagram © Tony Hall

a regular lattice that could be extended. What is happening here is the use of a theoretical model to explore the properties and consequences of a developing megalopolis that is an arrangement of a considerable number of closely packed and interacting cities. This could have an important practical application. Earlier in this chapter, several of the extensive conurbations of north-western Europe and north-eastern America were referred to. In rapidly developing countries, such as China at the time of writing, ever more extensive megalopolises are emerging. In China, the lower Yangtze around Shanghai–Suzhou and the Guangzhou–Shenzhen complex are prominent examples. To explore how this process of agglomeration could be a planned one could have considerable potential.

Comparison with examples from literature and practice

New towns and urban extensions

It is often said that there is 'nothing new under the sun' and town planning is no exception. Although nothing exactly on the lines set out here has been proposed before, let alone implemented, elements of the thinking can be traced back to the nineteenth century. In 1837 William Light produced his famous plan for then entirely new city of Adelaide in Australia. It had a rectangular plan $800\,m \times 2200\,m$, extending to a maximum of $2700\,m$ to the east, somewhat larger than the ped-sheds proposed here but still of a walkable scale. It had three satellite settlements, grouped together in what is now called North Adelaide, that were rather more walkable at approximately $800\,m \times 1500\,m$, $400\,m \times 1000\,m$ and $270\,m \times 500\,m$. What, however, was most significant then, and is still significant today, was the $600\,m$ deep park that surrounded the city. This permitted all residents to walk to an extensive and continuous expanse of parkland. It has also meant that, as the city has expanded, the first stage of construction after the original William Light plan was also within walking distance of parkland. (Whether, or not, that was Light's original intention is not the point.) When the railway came, it was not able to penetrate the built form and stopped in the park on the edge of the original built-up area, although a tramline did enter the original city and, in the early twenty-first century, was extended all the way through it.

With regard to the public transport-generated linear city, the credit for being the grandfather of them all is usually given to the nineteenth-century Spaniard, Arturo Soria y Mata. He proposed his tram-based Ciudad Lineal for Madrid in 1882. When built in 1892, it was a completely integrated, planned development around a new tramline. Originally planned to go for $48\,km$, only $5\,km$ were actually constructed. The buildings still exist today, although not the tramline. The buildings extended $200\,m$ either side of the line, well within walking distance. It ran circumferentially around the city, rather than outwards radially and would have depended on radial transport routes back to the city if its original ambition had ever been realised.

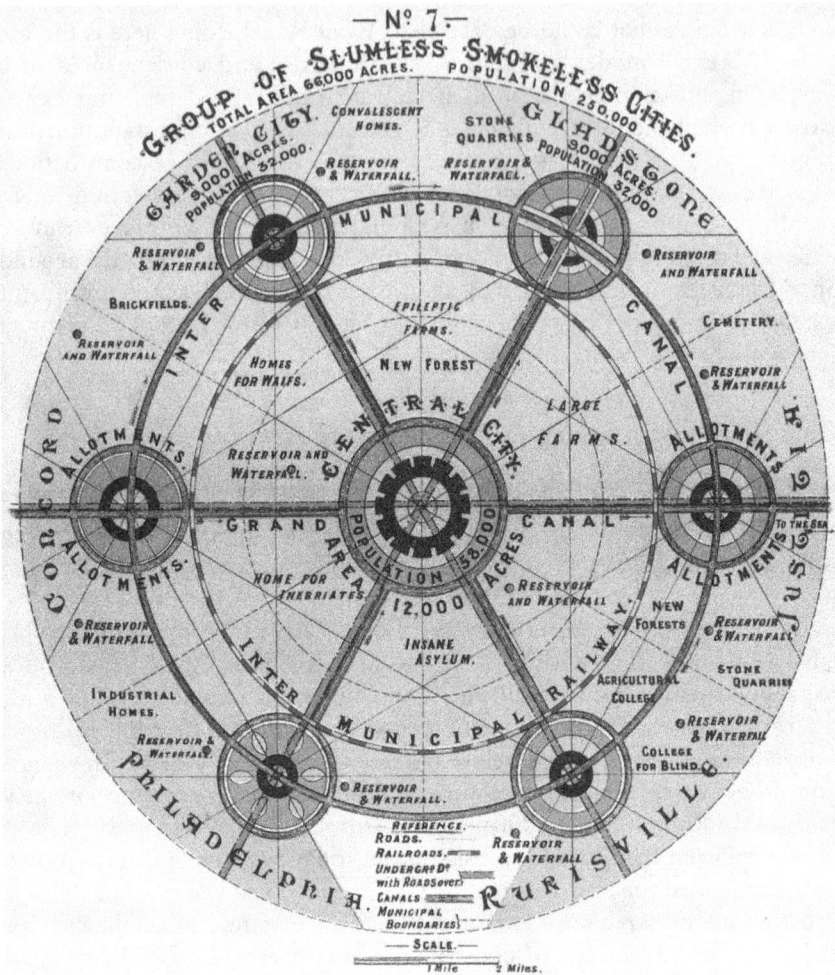

Figure 7.10 Ebenezer Howard's 'group of slumless and smokeless cities'

Source: Howard, 2003.

The first proposal to have a direct correspondence with the ideas put forward here and, indeed, the first to set out comprehensively and properly planned towns and cities in the modern sense, was Ebenezer Howard's *garden city* set out in his 1898 book *Tomorrow: A Peaceful Path to Real Reform* (Howard, 2003). His diagram for the standard *garden city* showed a circular form of 1000 acres, equivalent to an area of 405 ha and a radius of 1.14 km, somewhat larger than the ped-sheds proposed here but not excessively so. What is very significant in terms of the argument here was the diagram for 'smokeless cities' included in the first edition and reproduced in Figure 7.10. A 'central city', 1.8 times larger than the standard *garden city* was surrounded by a ring of the standard-size cities linked by roads and canals. Intriguingly, railways were to be used only for circular trips and they did not penetrate the built-up areas, unlike the roads and canals. On this basis, a complex of garden cities would have been able to expand radially and indefinitely, whether or not this was Howard's original intention. What are notable from the diagram are the green areas between the garden cities, which were to contain farms, quarries, recreational facilities and asylums. These were clearly to be functionally associated with the cities and have a definite correspondence to the *green enclaves* proposed in this book.

The special importance of Howard's work was that it was carried through into implementation, rather than just being ideas on paper. The first garden city to be built, Letchworth, had its central civic and retail areas adjacent to a railway station, with the original urban area being within, approximately, a radius of 1.3 km. (More recent development, however, extends 2 km from the centre.) The second garden city, Welwyn, built 20 km from Letchworth, had a substantial centre including a department store, other shops and civic buildings adjacent to one side of a main-line railway station with factories on the other. The original city was contained within a radius of 1.2 km. (The contemporary urban area now extends 2.7 km from the centre with a maximum of 3 km.) The points of correspondence between the ideas advocated here, and the two garden cities as built are the mixed-use centres on a railway line and urban areas of a manageable size, with a large proportion of the population being within walking distance of essential facilities.

During the latter part of the inter-war period of the mid-twentieth century, there was extensive house building by both the private and public sectors in Europe and North America. Although some of it was of interest in terms of the development of general ideas of town planning, this period did not produce examples that resonated clearly with the proposals of this book. This was not to happen until the construction of new towns in Western Europe during the 1950s. The story of the British new towns, and the ways in which they departed from the ideals of the garden city movement, is a well-known one. In particular, many were not built around railway stations, even though they all eventually acquired one a considerable time later. The French and Swedish new towns were more strongly influenced by the modern movement in architecture resulting in an emphasis on blocks of flats, many of which were high-rise in form, rather than houses and gardens. Where there was a point of correspondence to the ideas here was the relationship of the Swedish new towns to the city of Stockholm and its transport network. Unlike their British counterparts, which were intended, in theory if not in practice, to have a high degree of self-containment, the new towns built under the 1952 General Plan for Stockholm were clearly seen as satellite settlements of the main city. They were built around stations on new underground railway lines and were connected by them to the city centre. Residential densities were related to distance from the railway station. Blocks of flats, often high-rise, were provided within 500 m. Houses and gardens were limited to 10–15 per cent of the total dwelling stock and were located 500–1000 m from the station. A very important difference from the ideas presented here was that the new towns in Western Europe were all specially built directly by the state rather than being part of general planning policy applying to both public and private sectors.

Mention must also be made of the 1948 *Finger Plan* for Copenhagen. This proposed that the expansion of the city should be contained within corridors along radial suburban railway lines. The 'fingers', 1.0–1.5 km wide, would contain regional centres and employment concentrations in addition to the housing. The land between the 'fingers' would be *green wedges* approximating to the *green enclaves* proposed here. In the event, development was concentrated in two 'fingers', rather than the planned five, but the principle of restricting growth to corridors continued. The important points of correspondence were the protected *green* areas and the fact that this was a general long-term plan for all types of development. It was, though, actually implemented, if only in part.

Correspondence to the ideas proposed here became much greater during the 1960s and early 1970s. In 1962 in Britain, the county planning officer for Buckinghamshire, Fred Pooley, proposed the North Bucks New City (Pooley, 1966) on a site 70 km north-west of London, astride the main railway line (Ortolano, 2011; Berrett, 2014). It was to accommodate 250,000 people in 50 'townships' or 'villages' linked to each other, and to a very large central shopping and entertainment complex, by two monorail lines running in loops, as shown by Figure 7.11(a). (The two loops could be seen making a figure-of-eight shape although they did not intersect with each other.) The central shopping and entertainment complex would be immediately adjacent to the main railway line and be served by a new station. The 'townships' were to contain both flats and houses and gardens and, judging from the illustrations supplied at the time, they would have been at a reasonably high residential density. Examples are shown in Figure 7.11(b) and Figure 7.11(c). The city was not to be seen as 'suburban'. The monorail line would run to one side of each township and a main road linking it to the national motorway network to the other. The green areas inside the monorail loops would contain parks, schools and sports arenas. Light manufacturing industry was to be located at the extreme ends of the figures of eight. If the 'townships' are seen as 'half ped-sheds' then the correspondence with ideas here becomes very close, especially for the resulting 'green enclaves'.

An elevated monorail system was evaluated against other public transport systems and was seen as the best alternative. Monorail proposals were more common then than in later decades and fitted the futuristic atmosphere of much planning thinking at the time. They had, however, significant disadvantages, especially the high capital cost which would have had to be incurred almost entirely upfront. Monorails also have technical limitations regarding switching when compared with other track-based systems. Another criticism of the monorail loops was that, once complete, the city could not

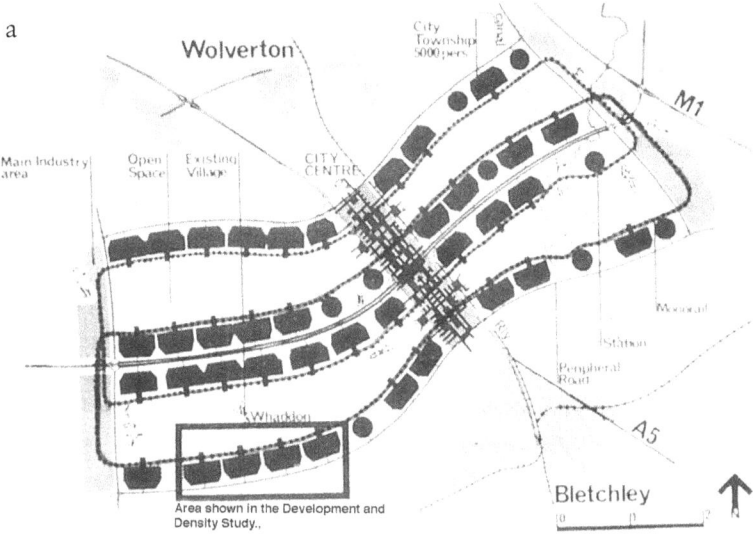

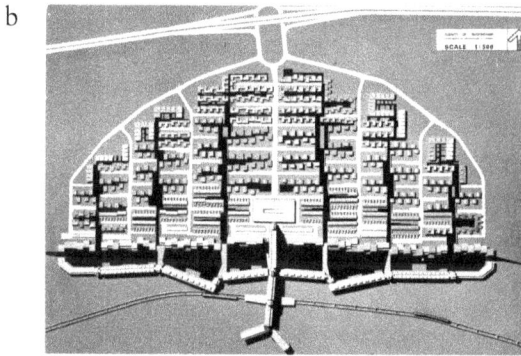

Figure 7.11 Fred Pooley's proposed city for North Buckinghamshire, UK: (a) The schematic plan for the proposed city, (b) and (c) a model of results of the study of residential density within the proposed 'townships'.

Source: Reproduced by permission of Brian Berrett.

easily be expanded, other than by building parallel loops. In the event, this design of the new city was not to be. The new city of Milton Keynes was subsequently built to the same size and on the same site. The fixed design with its high upfront costs did not prevail against the *flexible car-based grid* concept discussed at the beginning of this chapter and this was the pattern subsequently adopted for the new city (MKDC, 2014).

A similar design concept to the North Bucks New City was promoted by the Canadian aluminium firm of Alcan. *A Town Called Alcan* (Alcan, Cullen and Matthews, 1966) proposed four similar circular monorail circuits, linking both new and existing settlements, for *Solway* (near Carlisle), *Solent* (south Hampshire), *Redrose* (south Lancashire) and London. The interesting idea, for our purposes, was that they demonstrated how an expansion of the population for the areas could be accommodated by stringing new compact settlements along public transport lines. None of the ideas was, however, taken up.

One new town in Britain was, nevertheless, actually built on a similar public transport-loop principle. During the late 1960s and early 1970s, Runcorn, a town of 30,000 people in Cheshire, was expanded into a new town which had reached a population of 120,000 at the time of writing. As with the North Bucks New City, a figure-of-eight shaped monorail line, and also an alternative light rail facility, to link both existing and new settlements to a large central shopping and entertainment complex, were evaluated (RDC, 1967). The monorail and light rail ideas did not survive the preliminary technical investigations and were replaced by a dedicated busway following the same loop. The idea was for local centres to be spaced every 800 m along the busway with all the houses within a five minute walk (seen as approximately 400 m). Twelve local centres with surrounding housing were constructed, all accommodated within a 500 m radius. The busway continues to function to this day. The correspondence to the proposals here is close, but with two important exceptions:

- figure-of-eight circuits do not allow for expansion of the original town along public transport routes;
- it was a special public sector development sponsored by the government, not a general planning policy applied to all public and private development in the area.

It was, however, a genuine *beads-on-string* plan and one that did actually get built. Runcorn also showed what might have been possible at the North Bucks New City, which was proposed in approximately the same time period. Had the North Bucks monorail been replaced with a busway, as at Runcorn, its initial capital cost would have been substantially reduced and the bus would have been able to run to locations off the busway, also as at Runcorn. It is also likely that had both Runcorn New Town and the North Bucks New City been proposed some decades later, a light rail system, an idea which was by then was more fashionable, might have had a greater chance of selection.

The late 1960s also saw the first ideas for 'beads-on-string' that would link both new and existing settlements along existing railway lines. The Northampton, Bedford and North Bucks Study (Wilson and Womersley, 1965) accommodated growth in the sub-region that would have contained Pooley's original city along the existing railways lines; this idea had a certain correspondence to the Alcan proposals without their monorails. Much later, it was taken up and extended by Peter Hall and Colin Ward in their book *Sociable Cities* (Hall and Ward, 2014). Their new cities of *Mercia, Anglia* and *Kent*, shown in Figure 7.12, had all additional development in small settlements linked to each other, and to the existing towns and cities, by the existing railway lines. What is notable about these proposals is that they expressed general planning policies that could guide both ongoing public and private sector development in an incremental fashion over long time periods. Unfortunately, none of them came anywhere near being built and, therefore, subject to test by practical experience. It was to be another 30 years, in the 1990s, that planning thinking returned to these themes.

An interesting proposal in the early 1990s was the *Ecologically Sound Urban Development* project (Tjallingii, 1995) from the Netherlands by agencies of the Dutch government in conjunction with three local municipalities. It considered patterns of linkage, what it termed 'chains', for energy, waste, traffic and, as might be imagined for the Netherlands, water. It developed them into a 'guiding model' for a new city. Its form could be described as a *linear-radial* pattern comprising *fingers* of built-up areas approximately 600 m wide radiating out from a city centre and with green wedges in between. The principal difference from the model developed in Chapters 2 and 3 was that industrial areas formed whole *fingers* with the major roads and railways running though them, presumably on the basis that such areas would need to be served by heavier vehicles and would be less sensitive to environmental disturbance. What was very unusual, and very Dutch, was that the maximum extent of the city was to be limited by a maximum cycling distance, in this case 2.5 km. Although it was not explicitly stated, the implication appeared to be that additional cities would be built once this limit had been reached. Also proposed was an urban fringe (peri-urban) settlement design that bore a certain resemblance to the Breheny–Rookwood proposal, discussed in Chapter 6 and illustrated by Figure 6.6. Such a residential area located outside the boundary of the main city would be built around a tram stop. No figure was given for its actual width. It would be surrounded by green areas containing urban forestry and urban intensive agriculture, and parks containing both recreation and water facilities.

In the late 1990s, the British government set up an *Urban Task Force*, a working group chaired by the architect Richard Rogers, to find ways to 'bring people back into cities, towns and urban neighbourhoods'. Its report, *Towards an Urban Renaissance* (UTF, 1999), devoted part of its content to the question of the design of urban extensions to cities. It criticised the physically

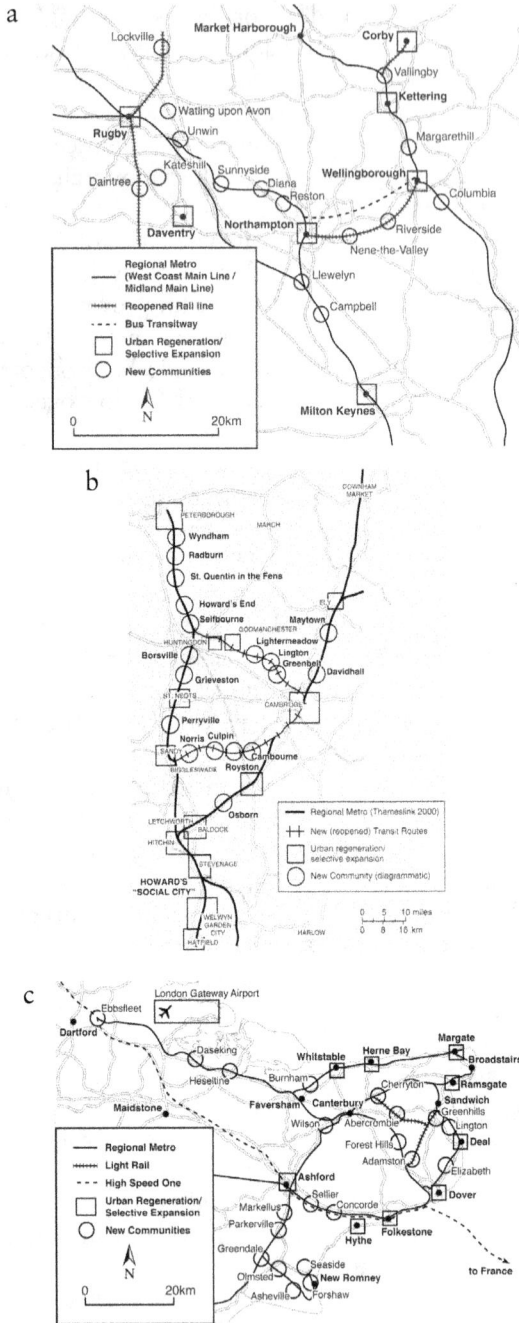

Figure 7.12 Peter Hall's 'cities of Mercia, Anglia, and Kent': (a) city of Mercia, (b) city of Anglia and (c) city of Kent

Source: Drawn by Professor Sir Peter Hall and reproduced by permission of Taylor and Francis.

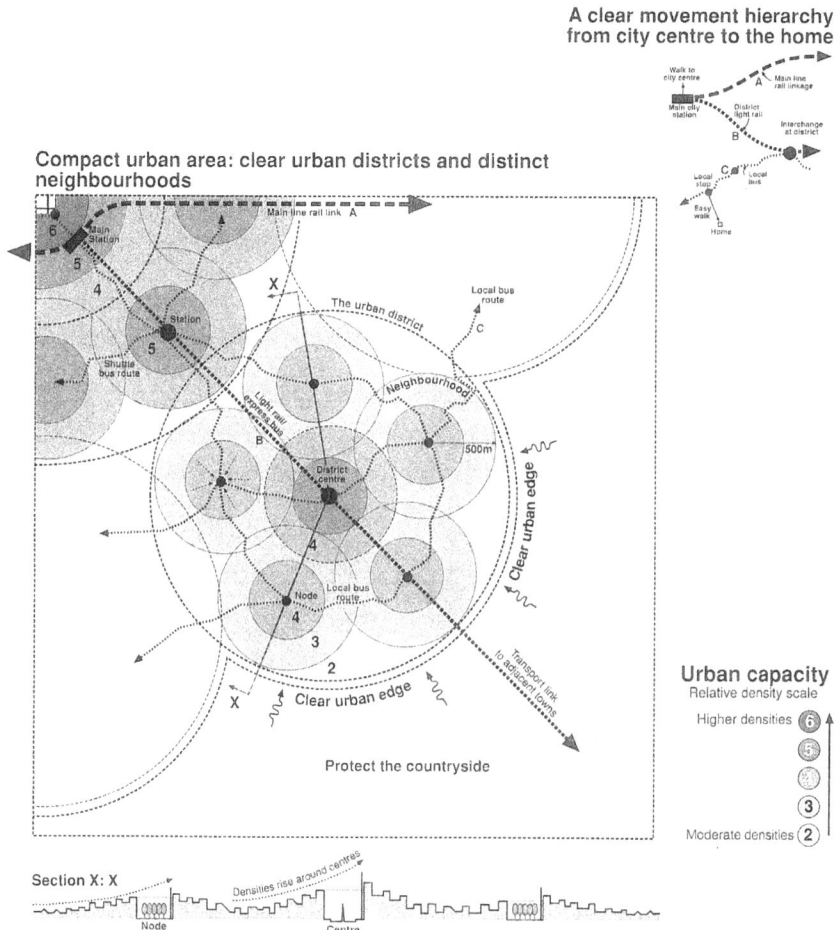

Figure 7.13 Diagrammatic proposal for city extension made in the 1999 Urban Task Force report

Source: Drawn for the 1999 Urban Task Force report by Andrew Wright, Architect, reproduced by permission

continuous incremental extension of urban areas (referred to in Chapter 3 of this book as *onion rings*) and proposed, instead, a systematic method of extension based on public transport corridors, districts and neighbourhoods as shown by Figure 7.13. 'Neighbourhoods' were a fundamental concept throughout the report and were seen as having a radius of five minutes walk, equivalent to 500 m. They had mixed-use centres with residential density reducing as distance from the centre increased. City expansion would take place around district centres located on radial transport corridors. 'Districts' would have a radius of 20 minutes walk and contain the 'neighbourhoods' which would surround the district centre. It was claimed that this would produce a 'hard urban edge', rather than the fragmentary erosion of the countryside, but exactly how this would work as the city expanded radially was, unfortunately, not worked up and clarified, that is, would the non-built-up areas be left without development or would they be filled in?

It would be possible, in theory, to incorporate this pattern into the overall framework of the theoretical model by replacing the 10 minute walk ped-sheds with the 20 minute walk 'districts', in effect extending the pattern started in the diagram in Figure 7.13. This arrangement would, though, depend on adequate bus circulation within each district. The first major difference between such a model and that developed in this chapter is that it would depend on a *track-based + local bus + walk arrangement* rather than just *track based + walk*. The second is that there would no longer be green areas within walking distance for all residents. The argument in the Urban Task Force report is also based on the number of people needed in a catchment area to support specific local facilities, in contrast to the approach argued here, that the fact that these requirements may vary over time should be recognised.

An example from the beginning of the twenty-first century has been the expansion of Perth in Australia. The Western Australian state government produced a design guide called *Liveable Neighbourhoods* (WPAC, 2004) which has already been discussed in Chapter 6. The guide was strongly influenced by the ideas of American New Urbanism and, in an Australian context, appeared remarkably progressive. Like the British Urban Task Force report, discussed above, it was based firmly on the idea of the 'neighbourhood', hence its title. The 'neighbourhoods' were to have a radius of a five minute walk, seen as 400–450 m, with a 'corner store' at its centre and the hope of a bus route. The minimal shopping facilities compared to the neighbourhood centres in the Urban Task Force report reflected the much lower residential density expected, 20 dph with a minimum of 15 dph, although the guide hoped for 30–40 dph close to town centres and railway stations. Neighbourhoods were shown in the illustrations in the guides arranged on an orthogonal grid around a district centre, which would, ideally, be located on a public transport line where available. Rear lanes for vehicle access to houses were envisaged, although not obligatory, and shops were required to have parking at the rear in order to create a street frontage. Compared to European practice, the specifications for the road widths were large, offering little apparent restraint for traffic and parking.

There has been considerable opportunity to implement the guide, not only because of the substantial growth in the Perth region in the early twenty-first century, but also because of the simultaneous expansion of the newly electrified suburban railway system, permitting *transit-oriented development*. Unfortunately, the results have been disappointing. The new railway lines have been commonly located within the median strips of motorways, making access to stations, and the placing of new district centres around them, difficult. The wide roads allowed by the guide have been taken full advantage of, thus spreading out the development and reducing walkability. The design of the houses is not covered by *Liveable Neighbourhoods* but by another code which permits the same very large air-conditioned mansions, with large integral garages and minimal private open space (Hall, 2010) as in the rest of the country. For the most part, therefore, new residential development around Perth has not turned out significantly different from the extensive car-based suburbs around other Australian cities (or for that matter the outer suburbs in New Zealand and North America). The only district that could truly be said to be New Urbanist in character is Joondalup, 25 km north of the city centre, as mentioned in Chapter 5. Here the railway line has been diverted away from the motorway and the houses are terraced, providing true street form. Unfortunately, even here the private open space around dwellings is near to non-existent (Hall, 2010).

Much clearer correspondence to proposals set out in this book, probably the closest of all, is to be found at the new settlement of Northstowe in England. This is a new small town of 10,000 dwellings located 10 km north-west of the city of Cambridge on a contemporary guided busway constructed between Cambridge and Huntingdon along the route of an abandoned railway line. (It approximates to 'Lington' in Peter Hall's proposals as shown in Figure 7.12(b).) The express service on the busway commenced in 2011. When Northstowe is complete, some express buses will divert from the busway to run through it on a dedicated local busway. (Other services will be able to bypass the town on the main busway.) There will be a town centre and two district centres, as can be seen from the master plan shown by Figure 7.14. All the housing will be within a short walk of the busway, usually 200 m but with a maximum of 500 m. Construction is by private developers working with the central government's Homes and Communities Agency. Residential densities approach 40 dph with 35–40 per cent of dwellings being affordable, that is, subsidised housing. The entire development is intended to meet a high standard of sustainability. Where this proposal does not reflect the ideas advanced in this book is in the lack of any other new settlements along the 25 km of the busway. This is unfortunate as it would then have been a real test of the beads-on-string idea. However, it would still be physically possible, in theory, to do this in the long term, should local planning policies change.

Other theoretical structures for large cities

The examples discussed so far have either been fairly small scale, for specific locations or both. What have other writers who have considered the ideal form of larger-scale cites and city regions had to say? The entire issue of theoretical city form was discussed by Kevin Lynch in 1961 (Lynch, 1961) and, given the significance of his writings generally, it is worth devoting some space to his conclusions. He wrote long before the pursuit of sustainability had risen to prominence and the goals he judged urban form against were

Figure 7.14 Master plan for the new settlement of Northstowe, UK, on the guided busway north of Cambridge, UK

Source: Image courtesy of Gallagher Estates, Homes and Communities Agency and Terence O'Rourke Ltd. © Terence O'Rourke Ltd 2012. All rights reserved. No part of this plan may be reproduced in any form or stored in a retrieval system without the prior written consent of the copyright holder. Base map reproduced by permission of the Ordnance Survey on behalf of HSMO. © Crown Copyright 2012 Terence O'Rourke Ltd Licence number AL100017826. All rights reserved

'choice', 'human interaction', 'cost', 'comfort', 'community participation', 'growth', 'adaptability', 'continuity' and 'imageability', the last being his own term. He considered, and rejected, what he called the 'dispersed sheet' – a low-density, non-directional layout, similar to Frank Lloyd Wright's *Broadacre City* (Wright, 1945). He saw this as essentially car-based, doing nothing to promote human interaction but creating issues of lack of identity. He then considered a 'galaxy' of more compact settlements arranged on a triangular grid. He noted that this would provide local centres and easy access to open country, as with the proposals here, but it would lack economic and social focal points and would not create a hierarchy of centres.

He then went on to consider three basic models of the city: 'core', 'star' and 'ring'. For the 'core' model, the whole city was constrained within a limited radius at a very high density. Although this would provide a strong visual image, and would be advantageous for social and economic interaction, it would come with high costs attached. If it were the only option, it would offer a very restricted range of habitats. In the 'star' form, the city would expand along radial routes from a single centre, a form that can be seen both in the historical development of urban form and, for a planned example, in the 1948 Copenhagen Finger Plan. Although Lynch saw it as having many advantages, particularly for transport, it posed problems for circumferential movement and could cause congestion at the centre. As a 'star form' city expanded, these problems would get worse and local districts would become more and more remote from the centre. The 'ring form' city had all the built area within a circular band, with open land within it and no dominant centre. The issues it presented would depend upon the size of the ring. (A large-scale example would be the Randstad in the Netherlands.) It would also avoid a congested centre, and facilitate circumferential movement but, nevertheless, Lynch considered it inflexible in dealing with change over time.

Intriguingly, Lynch briefly acknowledged the type of city form advanced here. He noted that the 'star form' could be developed along branching transport routes. However, he rejected it, with very little discussion, on the grounds that it may cause potential difficulties with circulation and confusion for travellers when trying to remember successive branchings. It is tempting to speculate, though, whether his conclusions might have been different if he had pursued the idea in greater depth.

What he did do was to develop his theoretical models further and recast them into four 'systems': 'linear', 'linkage', 'radial' and 'grid'. By 'linkage' he meant a distributed set of focal points, each with its own character, interlinked by an irregular, often triangular, network of paths, derived from the pattern of the baroque city. On the basis of a consideration of the advantages and disadvantages of these four 'systems', he then synthesised them into one 'composite model'. Unfortunately, he did not include a diagram to illustrate what it would look like and how it would work. It was based largely on the 'grid' and 'linkage' systems. There would be a grid of 'freeways' that would provide for the movement of private, ideally automated, vehicles and for bus services that would loop off it to serve settlements. A triangular network of 'arterial' streets, linking local centres, would be overlaid on the 'freeway' grid. Some centres would have central functions but the dispersal of central functions would be permitted or even encouraged. Densities would be low but not uniform. Areas of open land would be provided between the connected settlements and would contain 'pleasure ways' where people could travel for enjoyment.

What is notable about Lynch's ultimate vision of the structure of the city is that it is not fundamentally *transit oriented*. Although public transport is included within it, it does not determine the form – that role is taken by the private vehicle. However, where Lynch's view differs from others of the period, and from Milton Keynes as built, is in its emphasis on a strong visual character, not just for the arterials but also for the freeways, something that Lynch stressed in all his writings.

Hildebrand Frey (1999) also provided lengthy discussion of the theoretical models of the shape of cities. He reviewed all of Lynch's arguments from

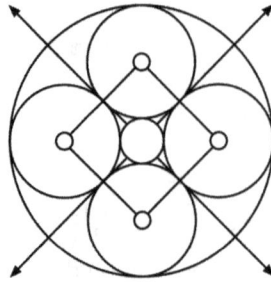

Figure 7.15 Hildebrand Frey's combination of 'neighbourhoods' into 'districts'

Source: Drawn by Hildebrand Frey and reproduced by permission of Taylor and Francis

nearly 40 years previously. He was sympathetic to the long established idea of the *neighbourhood*. He combined 'neighbourhoods' into 'districts', consisting of four 'neighbourhoods' around a district centre, as shown by Figure 7.15, much as those used in the Urban Task Force report (UTF, 1999) published at the same time (Figure 7.13). This provided a hierarchy of local centres, with the district centre located on a principal transport route. Frey's neighbourhoods had a 10 minute walk maximum radius which he interpreted as a 600 m distance. His district centres had a radius of 150 m and an area of 7 ha. This gave a maximum radius for the districts as a whole of nearly 2 km. He envisaged travel by local bus services within the districts, connecting the neighbourhoods to the district centre and, via a public transport node there, to inter-district travel. Both Frey and the Urban Task Force drew a circle around the *district*, appearing to imply that the land surrounding the neighbourhood boundaries was built up. If this were the intention, then this would result in a significant proportion of the residents being beyond walking distance of the district centre and another significant proportion being beyond walking distance of open country. For those without access to a car, these trips would have had to be made by local bus and, in this regard, both the Frey and Urban Task Force districts bore a strong resemblance to the 'small towns and new communities' proposed by Breheny and Rookwood (1993).

As with the Urban Task Force proposals, it would be possible, in theory, to incorporate this pattern into the overall framework of the theoretical model by replacing the 10 minute walk ped-sheds with the 20 minute walk 'districts'. As was remarked earlier, the first major difference between such a model and that developed in this chapter is that it would depend on a *track-based + local bus + walk arrangement* rather than just *track based + walk*. The second is that there would no longer be green areas within walking distance for all residents.

Frey went on to debate whole city models. Drawing heavily on Lynch, he compared the 'core city', 'galaxy', two variants on the 'star', 'linear city', 'regional city' (where towns and cities were arranged on a polycentric net) and 'satellite city', a system of smaller cities arranged in a circle around a larger one, very similar to Ebenezer Howard's proposal. To get to a quantitative basis for a comparison between them, he made assumptions about population density and considered two alternative city sizes. The sense of the discussion was concerned with an optimum size of city rather than a system that would facilitate indefinite expansion. There is merit in quoting Frey's conclusions in full:

> Overall, and under the assumption that all models accommodate a similar population and that all criteria are given equal weight, the core city scores worst, the linear city and the galaxy of settlements second worst, the star city is somewhere in the middle, and the satellite city and regional city score best. However, if the degree of containment, access to services and facilities, access to the countryside, environmental conditions and the potential for social mix, local autonomy and adaptability are given higher priorities, the core city clearly scores negatively in all aspects other than containment, the galaxy of settlements and the linear city are somewhere in the middle, the star city and satellite city score well and the regional city again scores best. If containment is given a high priority, then the compact city scores best, and the galaxy of settlements and linear city worst, as can be expected. With regard to the city-country relationship, the core city is problematic when larger than the central core of the star or satellite city, whereas all other city models score well.

He continues in his conclusions:

> Population densities and containment of the urban fabric become relative values when seen against access to provision centres and the open country, against environmental conditions, the potential for social mix and local autonomy and the degree of adaptability of the city to changing needs and conditions. The question of a sustainable city form is therefore changed into the question of a sustainable regional form as it becomes increasingly clear that the quest for sustainability has to take into consideration not only that of the city but also that of the countryside with which the city ought to have a symbiotic relationship.

Frey clearly valued areas of open land, equivalent to the *green enclaves* advocated here, but he also made clear his concern about how they might become fragmented. He was also concerned about how the built-up areas might become fragmented. Frey's concerns are well founded and need to be taken seriously. To an extent, the arguments for sustainable form do inevitably lead to a certain fragmentation, as can be seen from their exploration here. However, it is argued here that there are no adverse consequences if the overall design is properly handled. As with Lynch, Frey did not consider the precise form advocated here and so his views on it are not available.

Summary

The theoretical city model developed here has a number of very important properties.

*   The city can expand in a planned way while maintaining sustainable characteristics at all times. The city model allows for retrofitting of infrastructure as it expands.
*   The entire city is characterised by extensive green *non-built-up areas*, for want of a better term, called *green enclaves*. They can contain, in addition to large-scale recreational facilities, urban farms, market gardens catering to the needs of nearby residents, and educational ecological parks. They also provide space for the retrofitting of express public transport routes as the city expands.
*   Most remarkably, this theoretical city form appears to work perfectly for access by both walking and public transport while maintaining access for motor vehicles. The motor vehicles must keep to very low speeds in residential and retail areas but otherwise suffer little constraint.

There appears to be no apparent disadvantages. So why then has it never been tried? Its essential secret, and the principal difference between it and existing cities, is the presence of the *green enclaves*. To create them in practice would require a strong planning system guided by an explicit sense of purpose. In other words, it is not just a matter of promoting *transit-oriented development* but of a resolve to prohibit all development that is not *transit oriented*. The resulting city would then be both *green* and *robust*. It must be admitted that it would be most unlikely that an opportunity to create an entirely new city on these lines would present itself. However, it would have an application to the extension and intensification of existing cities and this will be addressed in Chapter 8.

References

Alcan Industries Ltd, Cullen, Gordon and Matthews, Richard (1966) *A Town Called Alcan*, Leicester: De Montfort Press.

Berrett, Bill (2014) *The Worlds' First Eco-city? The Proposal to Build a New City in North Buckinghamshire 1962*, privately printed.

Breheny, Michael and Rookwood, Ralph (1993) Planning the Sustainable City Region, in *Planning for a Sustainable Environment: A Report by the Town and Country Planning Association*, edited by A. Blowers, London: Earthscan, pp. 150–189.

Colin Buchanan and Partners (1966) *South Hampshire Study: A Report on the Feasibility of Major Urban Growth*, Ministry of Housing and Local Government, London: HMSO.

Frey, Hildebrand (1999) *Designing the City: Towards a More Sustainable Urban Form,* London: E & FN Spon.

Hall, Peter and Ward, Colin (2014) *Sociable Cities,* second edition, Abingdon: Routledge.

Hall, Tony (2010) *The Life and Death of the Australian Backyard,* Melbourne: CSIRO Publishing.

Howard, Ebenezer (2003) *Tomorrow: A Peaceful Path to Real Reform,* original 1898 edition with commentary by Peter Hall, Dennis Hardy and Colin Ward, London: Routledge.

Lynch, Kevin (1961 [1990]) The Pattern of the Metropolis, in *City Sense and City Design: Writings and Projects of Kevin Lynch,* edited by T. Banerjee and M. Southworth, Cambridge, MA: MIT Press.

MKDC, Milton Keynes Development Corporation (2014) *A Plan for Milton Keynes,* Introduction by Mark Clapson, Abingdon: Routledge.

Ortolano, Guy (2011) Planning the Urban Future in 1960s Britain, *The Historical Journal,* 54(2), pp. 477–507.

Pooley, Fred (1966) *North Bucks New City,* Aylesbury: Buckinghamshire County Council.

RDC, Runcorn Development Corporation (1967) *Master Plan,* Runcorn: Runcorn Development Corporation.

SEEPC, South East England Economic Planning Council (1967) *A Strategy for the South East,* London: HMSO.

Tjallingii, Sybrand (1995) *Ecopolis: Strategies for Ecologically Sound Urban Development,* Leiden: Backhuys.

UTF, Urban Task Force (1999) *Towards an Urban Renaissance,* London: E & FN Spon.

Webber, Melvin (1964) *Explorations into Urban Structure,* Philadelphia, PA: University of Pennsylvania Press.

Wilson, Hugh and Womersley, Lewis (1965) *Northampton, Bedford and North Bucks Study: An Assessment of Inter-related Growth,* London: Ministry of Housing and Local Government.

WPAC, Western Australian Planning Commission (2004) *Liveable Neighbourhoods Edition 3,* Perth: Government of Western Australia.

Wright, Frank Lloyd (1945) *When Democracy Builds,* Chicago, IL: University of Chicago Press.

8 Application to urban expansion and intensification

It would certainly be a remarkable opportunity if the occasion presented itself for the building of an entirely new city to the design set out in Chapter 7. Although the purpose of the exercise was, as emphasised, a theoretical one, to tease out certain important lessons, a city designed on these lines could still be built. Unfortunately, the opportunities to construct entirely new cities on empty sites are, in reality, very few. Examples around the world are generally limited to new capitals and the experience with them is not something that should be a guide to standard city building. Their design is distorted by the requirements, ambitions, and often vanity, of the governments concerned. The instructive examples of Letchworth and Welwyn Garden Cities in England in the early twentieth century have already been mentioned but they are of a 'town' scale of less than 100,000 population. For cities in excess of 200,000 population, aside from the new national capitals, probably the only example of a completely planned and free-standing large city, built on a greenfield site in the twentieth century, is that of Milton Keynes, also in England, which has also already been discussed in Chapter 7, and elsewhere, in this book. Nevertheless, the results obtained from the analysis of the theoretical model do have practical application and it is the intention of this book that it should make a useful contribution to practice. The practical applications come under two broad headings: urban extensions and urban intensification. However, before discussing them, it is first necessary to examine the principal differences between the theoretical model and planning practice.

Differences between the theoretical model and planning practice

When comparing the theoretical model with the actual development of urban areas around the world, both planned and unplanned, there are two principal differences that stand out. Firstly, the lack of a necessary provision of quality public transport routes within new build and, secondly, the continuous built infill between radial patterns of urban expansion, that is, no green enclaves. We will consider these in turn.

Provision of quality public transport routes

Although there are praiseworthy exceptions, more often than not cities expand without the incorporation of quality public transport routes within urban extensions at the time of construction and new satellite settlements can be built without such facilities. Even when such transport infrastructure is added later, this may be after a significant delay, sometimes many decades, with much additional expense being incurred when it is eventually built. Moreover, the new development may not then be purposefully designed around the public transport provision in order to ensure that it is properly integrated. The reason why delay or omission occurs is not difficult to discern. The capital cost is high. Developers can sell new property without access to it on the basis that people can access it by car. This, however, does not need to be the case. It ought to be one of the major differences between the properly planned and the unplanned city. In many developing countries the problem of the unplanned city can be clearly seen. Infrastructure follows on 'too little, too late' as it depends on the government to fund it in arrears. The argument is that, for the planned city, public transport infrastructure should be seen as a basic element of development, along with roads, sewers, water and electricity supplies. Their costs should all be incorporated within the costs of development. Different countries may have different methods for the collection and spending of the moneys involved but, whatever may have happened in the past, it is inconceivable that, in any contemporary situation, a residential area could be built without, say, sewers. So should the appropriate public transport infrastructure be included at the outset. Furthermore, this starting infrastructure is only the beginning – a minimum provision. As has been argued at many stages in this book, more will be needed locally to cope with the expansion of the city beyond the original urban area.

It was argued in Chapter 6 that *quality provision* implied a track-based facility. However, even with track-based public transport there is considerable flexibility with regard to both overall cost and to the phasing and upgrading of provision over time. At the cheaper end of the range, at least as far as capital cost goes, there is the dedicated busway as, for example, can be found in Runcorn in England and Brisbane in Australia. The next step up is the guided busway as, for example, in Cambridgeshire and Luton–Dunstable in England and Adelaide in Australia. As a city expands, a busway can be converted to include light rail as well, or the light rail to replace the buses, as long as this had been planned for when the busway was originally designed. Purpose-built light rail would be the next step up in capital cost. Light rail can be designed to operate jointly with heavy rail provision, a facility known as the tram-train or Karlsruhe model, after the city of that name in Germany. Tram-train operations are now to be found in a number of Western European cities. As the city expands, it would, therefore, be possible to start with a bus-based facility and then to upgrade to different rail-based types by stages.

The preferred scenario would be to ensure that land-use planning goes hand in hand with the planning of new light and heavy rail facilities or makes use of spare capacity on existing rail lines. In other words, new development should be located around strategically appropriate stations on existing and proposed lines and new lines should be designed with such development in mind. It is also possible, where the opportunity arises, to save on capital costs by reusing the formation of disused railways and restoring passenger services on lines that are freight only. All this is, after all, what proper planning should be about. In the context of flexible and comprehensive planning, the cost of always including quality track-based provision may not, therefore, be as extreme as might appear at first sight.

Green enclaves

The green enclaves are the other marked difference between the theoretical model and actual urban areas. However, the difference is not as extreme, on closer examination, as it might at first appear. Even in unplanned cities, as can be seen in many third-world examples, there are areas of low land value, such as flood plains of rivers, where building is difficult and with high risk. In planned first-world cities *green holes* in the urban fabric can be quite common. An interesting example can be found in Melbourne, Australia. The area illustrated diagrammatically by Figure 8.1 is a large green wedge that starts about 5 km from the city centre and then continues out for more than 15 km north-east along the line of the River Yarra to the boundaries of the urban area of greater Melbourne. It ranges in width from less than 500 m to 1500 m or more. The predominant land use is golf courses but

Figure 8.1 The green wedge along the Yarra River in Melbourne, Australia

Source: Diagram © Tony Hall

not exclusively so. It has remained un-built over primarily because of the landform not being the most suitable for development and also because of a long struggle, ultimately unsuccessful, to achieve a comprehensive green belt provision for greater Melbourne (Buxton and Goodman, 2008). However, the relevance to the argument here lies not in its history but in its dimensions and location in relation to infrastructure. To the south is a tramline and to the north a suburban railway line, both running roughly parallel to the edges of the green wedge (for station spacings see Table 6.1). The distance of both these track-based facilities from this edge is approximately 700–800 m, although in places this can increase to 1500 m. In overall scale, therefore, this green area corresponds to the green enclaves in the theoretical model. It even incorporates a motorway as retrofitted infrastructure.

The reason for the existence of these *green* areas in many cities bears some brief further examination. Many may arise from historic patterns of land ownership, often resulting in their eventual acquisition by a public authority. This is often the case for the larger public parks. What is very noticeable is that they tend to be in river valleys and flood plains. Historically, the land there was less desirable for building and, therefore, cheap. When it was not needed for industrial purposes, it was unlikely to have buildings on it, and so could be a preferred location for playing fields, which need a lot of space, and for public parks. As they are along the line of rivers, the parks and sports fields tend to come together in a linear agglomeration. Open areas may also occur where land is less desirable for building because the gradient is very steep, in practice on the tops and sides of hills. Existing cities can, and do, therefore have green enclaves, albeit not on the scale of the theoretical model, and they are often associated with physical features in the original terrain. This leads to the realisation that this aspect of theoretical model could be made easier to implement by 'going with the flow' of the pre-existing terrain.

An additional green goal

This realisation could be turned into a planning policy by adopting an additional goal within the overall goal of the pursuit of sustainability as already formulated. The additional goal would be that urban form should respect and enhance the pre-existing *natural* environment – terrain, water system, flora and fauna – the whole ecology. This would lead on to more specific criteria and plan objectives. One would be that certain physical features need to be free of development, for example flood plains and hilltops. The hilltops need to be free for aesthetic reasons as well as environmental ones. They can often be seen from afar and green ridges can create a sense of visual separation within an otherwise continuous built-up area. For the flood plains, there is the primary objective of managing floods but also the maintenance of habitats and biodiversity. This is in addition to their recreational value. Parks can be located on hilltops and in flood plains. Taken together, river

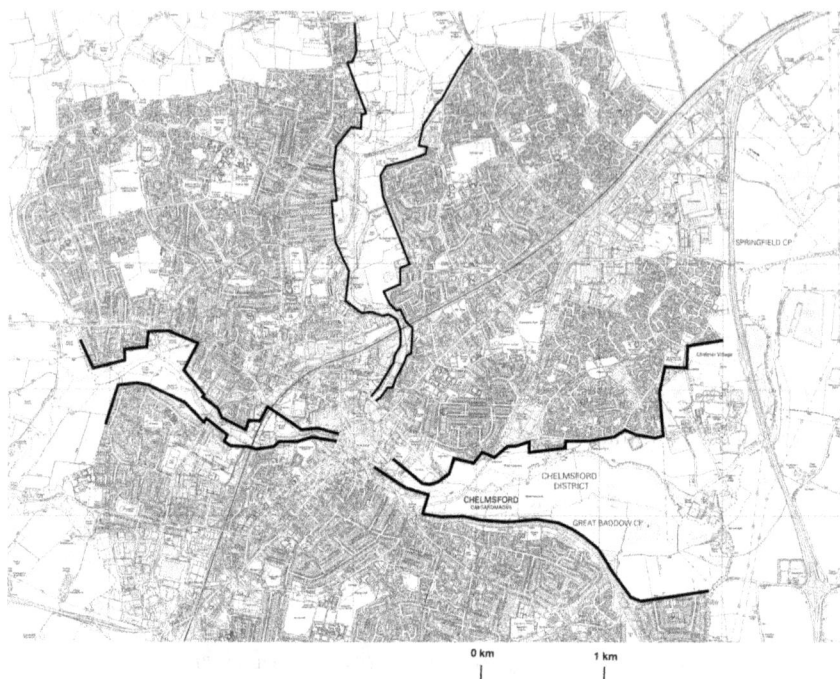

Figure 8.2 Green wedges within the urban area of the city of Chelmsford, Essex, UK

valleys can provide linear parkland incorporating sports fields and facilities and routes for longer distance footpaths and cycle ways. An example from the city of Chelmsford, UK, where three *green wedges* radiate from the city centre along the river valleys, is shown in Figure 8.2. This is for the same city as illustrated in Figure 3.3 but, whereas that diagram showed it in a rather critical light, Figure 8.2 illustrates a positive planning policy.

This additional sub-goal within the goal of the pursuit of sustainability could be seen as pursuing *robustness* within the *natural* environment equivalent to that for the physical environment proposed in Chapter 5. In other words, not just the urban form should be robust but so should the handling of the local ecology. The green enclaves are there not just to allow the retrofitting of infrastructure and permit ready access to open land for the inhabitants but also the proper conservation and stewardship of the local ecology. A decision to keep some areas free from development also carries, conversely, implications for where building could take place, which is what planning should be about. The difference between the theoretical model and a planned city might not be as difficult in practice as might be imagined, more a matter of degree.

Green enclaves versus green belts

The emergence of green belts as a planning idea dates largely from the first half of the twentieth century, although its implementation had to wait until the middle of that century (Amati, 2008). The most notable and widespread implementation of the concept has been in Britain and, within this same country, the most remarkable example has been the Metropolitan Green Belt (MGB) surrounding Greater London. What is remarkable about it is its sheer scale: an inner radius of approximately 20 km and an outer one of 50 km, extending to 60 km in places. It contains not only a wide range of land uses but also some quite large towns and numerous smaller settlements. The size and content of such a planning designation has provided much fuel for debate about its purpose. However, the task here will not be to discuss particular examples of green belts worldwide, or their detailed histories, but to try to unpack the concept in a way that might complement the findings from the theoretical model.

Green belts possess two fundamental characteristics by definition:

- they are areas of land where only minimum (although not necessarily zero) development is permitted;
- they have an annular shape, that is, form a belt surrounding an urban area.

Much debate has always surrounded their purpose. They have appeared to represent many things to many people and to possess multiple functions at one and the same time. Their critics may portray this as a confusion of roles but this is unfair. It is a theme of this book that specific patterns of settlement form may have multiple advantages and, where this occurs, they are to be considered robust and are to be recommended. Where there are patterns of urban form that result in direct conflict with goals, then those patterns may need to be discouraged through the planning process. However, real progress can be made by resolving apparent contradictions between the goals and designing urban form that offers an optimum solution. The issue is, when a particular urban form allows the pursuit of a variety of goals that all pull together, are they symbiotic?

For green belts, let us first examine the principle of minimum development. At least three planning purposes have often been advocated:

- preventing urban areas coalescing;
- provision of space for outdoor recreation;
- protection, even preservation, of areas of countryside.

Prevention of coalescence needs to be seen as a separate purpose as there are examples of large regional parks being retained within large conurbations formed by the merging of towns and cities, that is, provision for recreation and limited countryside protection occurring within coalesced urban areas. The arguments in support of it are, though, rarely made explicit. One of the most important reasons is to allow space for the retrofitting of infrastructure, an argument made at some length elsewhere in this book. The other two purposes may, of course, be pursued in areas other than green belts. Their association with green belts arises from two other ideas:

• urban areas are advantaged by having protected areas adjacent to them;
• the advancing edges of urban areas pose the most pressing threat to the countryside.

What then is actually being protected? To be realistic, it must be admitted that a great deal of the local political pressure for the creation and retention of green belts comes from those living, or hoping to live, within their boundaries who see themselves advantaged by the protection from development they afford. However, there are, and always have been, more substantial planning arguments. There are a number of facets of the idea of the *countryside* that might merit protection. A number of items can be listed – landscape aesthetics, other cultural associations, biodiversity, food production and tourism. Although in the mid-twentieth century all these items might have been seen as symbiotic, experience was to reveal conflicts between them. Agricultural innovation has reduced biodiversity. Tourism has damaged both biodiversity and agriculture, and so on. Choices have had to be made and the degree of protection afforded has entered the debate. The issue of the degree to which each item should be protected has been especially challenging and could result in great complexity in decision making. However, what has become the key point in the retention of green belts is that, although it would not be possible to achieve 100 per cent protection of all of the items at the same time and in the same place, selected combinations, with varying degrees of protection, could be made to work in different locations. The evidence for this can be found in the British context where the green belt has been alive and well as a planning designation after over half a century of implementation. The extensive area of a green belt surrounding a fairly large town or city has made it possible to accommodate different items in different locations at the same time. There can, for example, be nature reserves, areas for horticulture, areas for outdoor sports and so on. There may even be locations where, as in the very extensive example of the MGB, few of the items may be protected, if at all. However, this does not invalidate the green belt as a wider concept and as a planning designation.

What is more significant for the argument here is the annular shape. It could be seen as arising from two additional objectives:

• containment of the urban area within fixed boundaries;
• maximum accessibility of the open area to the contained urban area.

The idea of a growth boundary completely surrounding a town or city may reflect intentions that the urban area so contained should not grow outwards. The implication, either implicitly or explicitly, is that either the population should not increase or that residential density should increase to accommodate a growth in population. The challenge that often arises is that either instead of, or in addition to, an increase in density, the pressure of growth within the contained urban area 'jumps' the green belt and continues on the other side of it. This has been the case with the MGB. In spite of its great extent, the growth pressure extends over the whole of Southeast England to a radius of at least 100–150 km. One implication of this phenomenon is that issues of containment and density need to be addressed on a regional, or at least sub-regional, scale. (For a discussion of the implications of this argument for the policy of *growth boundaries* as applied to some urban areas in North America and Australasia, readers should turn to Chapter 9.)

Regarding the intentions of the green *belt* as typified by British practice, it would be possible to adopt a more spatially flexible approach locally. Coalescence of urban areas can be prevented by local designations – by *strategic gaps* placed as and where required. The theoretical model developed in Chapter 7 showed that other shapes beside green belts can deliver even greater proximity of open land to built-up areas. The problem for the green belt concept is not the idea of a designated area of minimum development but in its annular shape.

Interpretation of the ped-shed radius

In Chapters 6 and 7, the ped-sheds are by represented by circles in the diagrams illustrating the theoretical model. As might be imagined, this is not meant to suggest an overly literal interpretation in practice. The 800 m radius should be seen not as a sharp boundary but a general indicator of a maximum easy walking distance. It is advanced as a rule of thumb based on the assumption that the average person can walk 800 m in approximately ten minutes and that the average person is willing to walk for up to that time as a maximum for most purposes such as walking children to school, shopping or finding a café. As was stressed in Chapter 6, it is firstly a maximum rather than an ideal, and secondly it is a broad estimate of the likely preferences of the average person. Taking a different figure of, say, 600 m or 500 m would still maintain the essential principles derived from the theoretical model: the green enclaves and accessibility based on walking plus quality public transport.

There are several other reasons why it should not be taken as a hard and fast rule. A simple radius drawn from a centre point gives an 'as the crow flies' distance and does not give an accurate indication of the actual distance that would need to be covered by walking along streets or footpaths that rarely run straight along the radius. A more accurate measure is the *isochrone* based on the true walking time along existing or proposed routes. In addition, it does not take into account the ease of walking, which will be affected by different gradients and surface textures, nor does it take into account the notion of psychological or perceived distance. It is known that people will be prepared to walk further if they sense they are heading towards a clearly defined common destination, such a railway station, particularly if it is a known distance and for a fixed daily purpose.

There will also be physical constraints on the shape of the ped-sheds arising from natural features such steep hills and rivers and barriers created by existing infrastructure, such as railway embankments and cuttings. For actual development schemes, the outer boundary of the buildings on the ground will not, therefore, be a perfect circle. However, that does not mean it cannot be deduced on a rational basis. It will still arise from a study of easy walking routes and of natural barriers.

The same arguments will apply to the actual layout of the mixed-use core of the ped-shed. A 100 m radius has been suggested as a rule of thumb for minimum provision of local facilities but its actual shape and size will depend on pre-existing physical features and local socio-economic circumstances, which may change over time.

Application to urban extensions

Although the opportunities to construct entirely new cities on empty sites may be very limited, the criteria derived from the theoretical model can still be applied to urban extensions, a far more frequent occurrence. Across the world, towns and cities and whole city regions tend to expand continuously, the point made in Chapter 3. This expansion will continue to place additional loadings on to the existing infrastructure, as was also observed in Chapter 3, and this is something that cannot be avoided if the urban area is to expand. What this book argues is that, when planning new development, space should be allowed for the retrofitting of infrastructure. If this is done, then policy should not prevent the new extensions from being laid out along public transport lines. The quality public transport lines can then branch out, and green enclaves be created between them, as in the theoretical model.

A practical method

In attempting to extract a practical method, what the argument of this book, in particular the discussion of the theoretical model, provides in terms of guidance for the physical planning of urban extensions is two-fold:

- a rational stepwise method or toolkit for their location and design;
- the idea that they should be designed to respond to growth over time.

A step-by-step method could be set out as follows:

1   The first step would be to identify an existing, or proposed, track-based public transport facility running radially from the existing urban area that could accommodate additional station stops. If necessary, a completely new route, to be financed in part from the proceeds of the development, would be proposed.
2   Locations for new station stops that could serve as the centres for new settlements would be identified on the basis of the suitability of the surrounding land for development in terms of its landform and other environmental constraints. These locations would not be the same as those for park-and-ride and low-intensity commercial and public facilities, which would have their own station stops.
3   A limit to the extent of development of the maximum walking distance of each station stop (e.g. 800 m) would be established. No major development would be allowed beyond this limit.
4   An area to accommodate high-intensity mixed-use development would be identified around and above the station, to be closely integrated with it in three dimensions.
5   New major roads would be aligned outside, but connecting to, the new settlements.
6   As more land for development was required, so sites for additional settlements of the same type would be identified along the transport corridor.

A flexible approach to growth

Guidance on the design of the physical form of the new settlements should not only reflect urban design principles that convey both a sense of place and high environmental quality, but should also provide a flexible response to growth in the very long term. The design and layout should be robust. Not only would there be a variation in residential density within each settlement (higher at the centre–lower at the edge) but it could vary between settlements (higher towards the existing urban area–lower at a distance from it). The actual density levels within and between the settlements could be expected to change over time. The same would go for the size of the mixed-use centres around and above the stations. They may start out as just very local ones, with a limited range of facilities serving a low-density ped-shed. Residents would travel to other centres, most likely in the existing city, for other services. However, over time, as many settlements grow up along the transport corridor, so one or two of them might grow into much more substantial centres serving a number of settlements in the corridor.

There is also the issue of the relationship of the radius of the ped-shed to the size of the urban area being expanded. The theoretical model developed in Chapter 7 addressed the idea of the city with a radius of 10–20 km but the same lessons derived from it could be applied to a small town with much smaller dimensions. In such circumstances, a diameter of 1600 m might be seen as excessive for new settlements built as an extension to the town and a 400 m radius, 800 m diameter, would likely be more appropriate. (The 20 minute walk radius of the *districts* proposed by Frey and by the Urban Task Force, as discussed in Chapter 7, would be even more disproportionate in size for town expansion.) It would also be physically possible to start with a radius of 400 m and expand the size later by up to another 400 m, that is, an 800 m radius. This would require the layout of streets and blocks to be designed to be extendable in line with principles expounded in this book. The obstacle to taking this approach, however, may be of a local political nature as the expansion would be likely to be opposed by the inhabitants of the first stage.

Examples of outcomes

This leads to two types of approach which may be seen either as alternatives to, or as two stages in, a very long-term process, depending on local circumstances. The first type is the location of one or two residential ped-sheds of, say, 4000–5000 dwellings, 1 or 2 km apart along a railway line or other, track-based public transport facility. These *new settlements* would have a central mixed-use core, primary school and other local services but would depend on the adjacent town or city, that is, the urban area that is being extended, for higher order services. If there is little pressure for further expansion from the city in this direction then this might remain the pattern for a time period of several decades. If strong pressure for expansion were to re-emerge after this period, then additional new settlements could be built beyond, or between, those already constructed.

Figure 8.3 shows one possible result of applying this method to the extension of an existing urban area. In this case, there is an existing railway line leading out of the city. A new station has been established on the line with a new settlement of maximum 800 m radius surrounding it. There is a mixed-use centre, with streets and urban spaces, within approximately 100 m radius of the station. Residential density declines with distance from the station. A pattern of intersecting suburban streets and public open spaces is maintained, but not on a rigid orthogonal template. The schools are located on the edge of the settlement so that their playing fields can extend into the surrounding open area. The new settlement is connected to a nearby motorway (not shown) and by local roads to the existing urban area.

There are, of course, many other possibilities and some are illustrated schematically by Figure 8.4. The public transport link could be provided by a guided busway or light rail facility instead of heavy rail. In parts of the world which are already highly urbanised, the new settlement may fit within gaps between several existing ones. In some cases, the new settlement may extend or incorporate an existing small one. For example, there may

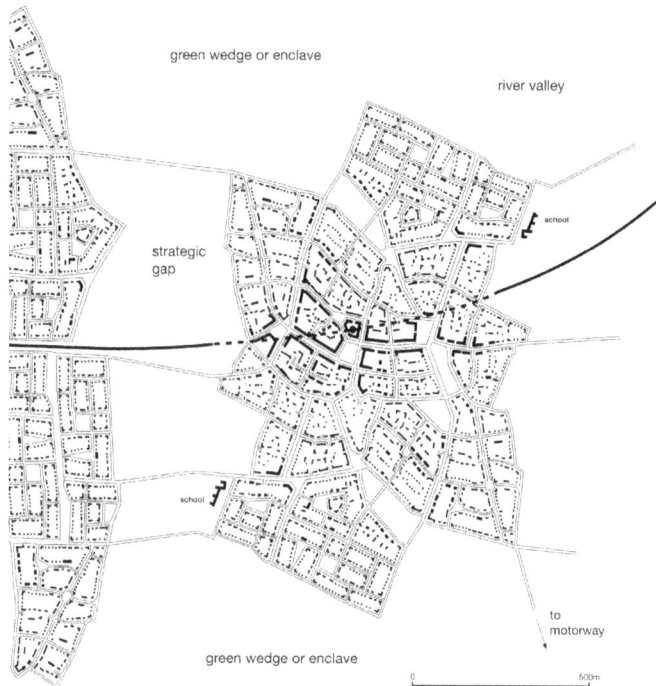

Figure 8.3 A representation of a possible application of the theoretical model to the extension of an existing urban area. In this example, a new 800 m radius settlement surrounds a new station on an existing railway line

Source: Diagram © Tony Hall

be the opportunity to build a new settlement on one side of a railway line complementing an existing one on the other and sharing its existing station. One new settlement could contain a new university campus with a university hospital; another could contain a park-and-ride facility and commercial uses. Some would be primarily residential with just local services, while others could incorporate a significant local shopping centre with higher-density housing.

One interesting observation is that expansion of large cities and city regions on this basis blurs the distinction between urban extensions and free-standing new towns. The ped-sheds are not exactly entirely free-standing settlements as they have a direct functional link to the existing urban area. On the other hand they are physically separated both from the existing city and from each other and they can facilitate a new pattern of local centres. As the extension grows, some of these centres may grow to become the equivalent of a town or city centres in their own right with neighbourhood centres in nearby ped-sheds associated with them. The approach is robust in the long term.

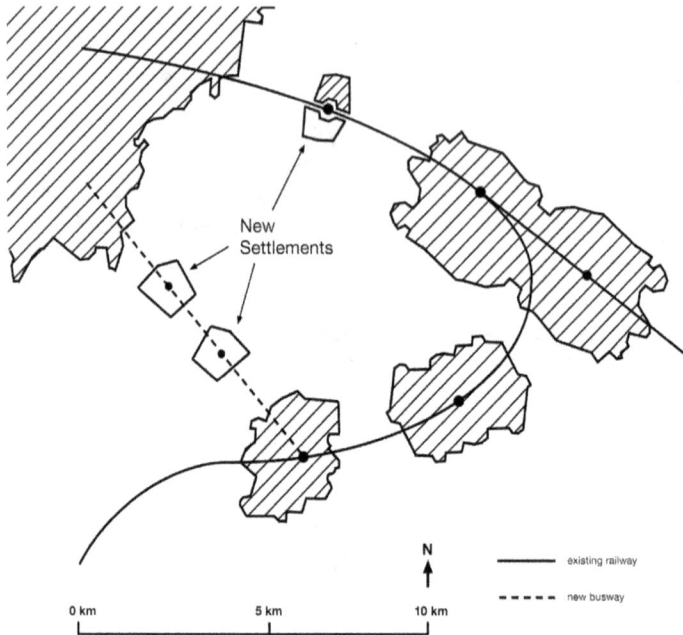

Figure 8.4 A hypothetical example showing some possible ways of providing new settlements as urban extensions following the theoretical model. As examples, new ped-sheds are shown along a new busway connecting existing urban areas. A new 'half ped-shed' complements an existing settlement on the other side of an existing railway station

Source: Diagram © Tony Hall

What about employment?

At this stage some readers may be wondering about employment. Surely, it is centrally important and has a significant impact upon urban form. Why has there not been more discussion and specification of its spatial requirements? The first answer is that it is the activity that probably changes the most in the long term. The story of the rise and fall of the manufacturing industry in western countries, with its immense physical as well as economic impacts, is too well known to need repeating here. The different phases in its growth and development and its subsequent rise in many Asian countries are also important stories, as is the persistence of service and knowledge-based economies. Although it is tempting to discuss these very interesting stories in detail, to do so would take up much space and would be a distraction from the main theme of this book. The main theme, as applied to this topic, is how the proper planning of the long-term physical structure of towns and cities can facilitate, and avoid obstructing, growth and change in employment, given that it can change massively, both quantitatively and qualitatively, within just a few decades.

The second answer is that predominantly residential ped-sheds would not be dormitory suburbs but contain mixed-use cores and other services outside the cores, all providing local jobs. Although there would be variation between ped-sheds, some having, say, much retailing and others only a minimum, there would always be some service employment. Moreover, it would be easy to travel to employment opportunities in neighbouring ped-sheds. Were a requirement to arise for a large manufacturing plant served by heavy goods vehicles, it could be accommodated by the construction of a new non-residential ped-shed. Its employees would be able to travel to work by public transport as well as private car. As long as design qualities and characteristics were maintained, if the plant declined or closed the ped-shed could be converted to a predominantly residential one while maintaining sustainability and quality of life. The same would apply to large distribution facilities, hospitals and educational institutions, all of which may be subject to significant changes in their design requirements over time as a result of technological and social change.

Application to urban agglomeration

In Chapter 7 there was some discussion of how the theoretical model might handle combinations of expanding cities of up to a 20 km radius. It was found that there was considerable advantage in leaving green space between them although they could continue to be connected by urban corridors, as illustrated diagrammatically by Figure 7.9. It was suggested that this could have practical application where there was pressure for cities and towns to merge together in a megalopolis stretching, possibly, for hundreds of kilometres. Such areas exist in western Europe, north-eastern USA and in many parts of the Pacific seaboard of Asia, where they are an increasing phenomenon at the time of writing. The model developed in this book could, therefore, prove very useful in pointing the way to managing such urban agglomerations and providing a rational basis for planning them. This would require the prior identification of:

- a high-quality intercity public transport line connecting each pair of expanding urban areas;
- large-scale green enclaves between the existing expanding urban areas where development will not be permitted, except for intercity transport corridors without intermediate access;
- where appropriate, an urban corridor, or linear city, between each pair of expanding urban areas that can be developed on a beads-on-string basis;
- all as part of a long-term (e.g. over 50 years) strategy.

Application to urban intensification

For a wide range of reasons, especially those connected with the pursuit of sustainability, planning policies and arguments in many parts of the world call for higher residential densities. Nevertheless, increasing the residential density in existing suburbs can be a controversial and challenging affair. Commercial pressures encourage it as the city grows but existing residents may resent the change to the nature of their surroundings. This opposition may be partly on aesthetic and amenity grounds but it can also be on the basis of the impact on the existing infrastructure, which may not be redeveloped in a manner synchronised with the increase in the number of dwellings or may not even happen at all. Matters are best handled if the infrastructure is dealt with in a planned manner with due attention to proper standards of urban design. The problem in most cities is that the process can be indiscriminate and, as a result, often uneven. The theoretical model can be of assistance in providing a rational planning basis for handling increases in residential density and associated infrastructure provision.

The first point that needs to be recognised is that high density should not be seen as an end in itself. Although fulfilling some important policies, it has its own disadvantages. The higher the density, the costlier is the construction. It is not advantageous, in itself, to have apartments instead of houses. It can work against the pursuit of sustainability, for example by increasing the consumption of energy. In addition, in any urban context there will be limits to the density that can be achieved. It is constrained by housing mix, external space needs and local scale and form. The term *high density* can posses a wide range of meanings. The 12 houses per acre (30 dph) of the garden city movement (Unwin, 2013) would be seen as high in comparison with the density in many existing suburban areas around the world. On the other hand, there is the 100 dph, or more, found in city centre locations in comparison with which the garden city ideal is very low density. However, high density is just as much about lifestyle, physical form and sense of neighbourhood. *Intensity* is a better term because it is as much about activity, social interaction, as just a quantitative measure. It is about creating the quality of life and vitality that makes urban living desirable. Density without intensity does not work. It does not feel comfortable, just squeezed. The physical design should deal with the needs of more compact urban living.

There are a number of questions that need to be addressed in devising a planning method to deal with these matters. What are the barriers to achieving high density? What has to give in order to raise density? How can planning policies place a limit on density between *high* and *too high*? How can planning implementation ensure that the finished product bears out the liveability advantages of high density in theory? Finding a solution in practice can be greatly assisted by devising locational principles for different levels of intensity of development. Their basis should be that the intensity of new development should reflect both the existing surroundings and the level of accessibility.

In addition, it follows from the emphasis on physical form argued in this book that the treatment of density issues in planning policy should not just specify the location of more intensive development but should link through to more detailed physical design. Planning policy should give guidance on the physical nature of the different levels of intensity that should be permitted in different locations. In pursuit of this, *intensity* can be expressed by a number of factors, including three-dimensional physical parameters, recognising the importance of the complexity of form and interaction of activities:

- density (persons, rooms, floorspace, dwellings / hectare);
- height (storeys, gross, to eaves);
- private open space;
- public open space;
- quantity and nature of vehicle storage;
- plot ratio;

and it can also incorporate all aspects of urban design, including the public realm. The point is that all of these should be planned for at the same time and in relation to each other.

In practice, the patterns of the interaction of the variables governing degree of intensity can be resolved into a number of distinct levels. For example, three levels could be as follows.

- High intensity:
  - full range of uses;
  - spatially mixed uses, overlapping in three dimensions;
  - higher buildings, generally four storeys;
  - residential form as flats or patio housing;
  - residential densities in excess of 40 dph;
  - townscape contained by buildings;
  - communal parking, visitors in public parking;
  - public open space as pocket parks.
- Medium intensity:
  - uses predominantly residential in area but still mixed;
  - residential densities 25–40 dph;
  - height normally two storeys, maximum three;
  - flats used to achieve design objectives, such as turning corners;
  - detached, semi-detached and terraced types;
  - house-and-garden form, private open space;
  - townscape contained by buildings and trees;
  - parking within curtilage or small, shared provision;
  - public open space as parks and playing fields.

- Low intensity (as medium intensity, except):
  - height one to two storeys, exceptionally three;
  - residential densities below 25 dph;
  - all parking with curtilage;
  - townscape contained by trees;
  - detached house types predominate.

These three levels are just examples. There could be a wider range with more, and different, intermediate levels, as might meet the requirements of local circumstances. However, the method is more important than the actual quantities expressed. What is significant is where this method leads us. It is not content to stop at the simple quantities of, say, residential density and building height, but leads on through the identification for each level of a *package* of parameters with particular values. This can lead us on again to the identification of particular morphological types, or examples of urban tissue, associated with each *package*. We are talking here about building types, street widths and proportions, planting and paving, amongst many other things. The significance is in the way that they all hang together. This can then interface directly with the instruments and policy vehicles used to guide and control urban form with physical planning, such a briefs, frameworks and design guides (Hall, 1996, 1997, 2007). Local values can then come into play to express requirements through *character areas* by which a sense of place may be achieved in particular localities. Unfortunately, space does not permit a further expansion of this important and interesting theme here, as it would require another book. (The reader may wish, however, to turn to the author's other work: Hall, 2007, 2008). To summarise, the possession of a rational basis for locating different levels of urban intensification permits the expression of these levels in terms of types of form and thence their incorporation into instruments of physical planning.

Robust layout of new residential development

This takes us to the need to look in more detail at the design of urban form at the level of resolution of the urban tissue, that is, the arrangement of urban blocks and streets in new developments. Chapters 4 and 5 showed how a goal-driven approach to the design of urban form for the long term leads to a convergence on the form of the perimeter block with low-rise, shallow-plan buildings and active frontage to slow speed streets. Such results are not new and are to be found in an extensive corpus of writing on contemporary urban design. It is, indeed, fortunate that the urban design principles that can be deduced from goals of sustainability and quality of life, as explained in Chapter 4, are also those that are, at the time of writing, widely accepted in professional circles. They are also ones that give guidance on the physical form that exhibits the necessary robustness.

The point that remains to be discussed now is how this also can be informed by the theoretical model and how this might help in achieving a flexible approach to changes in urban intensification over time. Just as at the citywide level of resolution, local robustness will arise from the design of the space between the buildings. At the level of the urban tissue, we are talking about significant green space to the rear of dwellings within the perimeter block layout. Leaving significant un-built areas can accommodate recreation, the needs of the environment and for the retrofitting of infrastructure, and allow for these to change over time.

The residential areas should be designed so that they can accommodate higher residential densities over time with minimal disturbance. Where the initial development is at a comparatively lower density, the way to do this is to have a vision of what the urban form would look like at higher densities while, at the same time, meeting all the planning goals. One can then work back from this to envisage design of the same area at the lower density, and also the stages in-between. One point that arises immediately is ensuring that the quantity of local public open space serving the needs of the surrounding dwellings (as opposed to strategic public open space, such as playing fields, that would be handled within the green enclaves) would be sufficient to provide for increased residential densities over time. The next point is that it is helpful to begin with fairly large urban blocks, say 80–110 m in width, as a basis for design, even though smaller ones may emerge over time. As an example, Figure 8.5 illustrates how matters could be handled for a 100 m × 100 m block. The actual size of the block and the dwelling types in practice would vary according to local circumstances; what matters is the general way of proceeding. Figure 8.5(a) shows such a block at low density, with detached houses laid out in a perimeter block form at 12 dph. Even when starting with such a low density it is important to consider the implications of possible intensification over time and develop planning policies accordingly. Were there to be few controls applied, the un-built centre of the block could be lost to either over-large houses or sporadic unplanned backland infill. Paradoxically, this would make intensification harder to achieve in the long term. If proper design principles are maintained, in particular the perimeter block form and green interior of the block, increasing densities can be handled in a planned manner. Figure 8.5(b) shows a block of the same size that has had a road added through the middle to create two 50 m × 100 m blocks. Use of terrace houses and corner types raises the density to the garden city ideal of 30 dph (Unwin, 2013) while maintaining the perimeter block form. This is not the same as unplanned infill. However, there can be much advantage in maintaining the larger block size in pursuit of a higher-density level. Figure 8.5(c) shows an alternative approach where the 100 m × 100 m perimeter block is maintained but the use of terrace houses together with flats to turn the corners raises the density to a range of 45–70 dph, depending on the size of flats, around 50 dph on average. In Figure 8.5(d) the use of flats

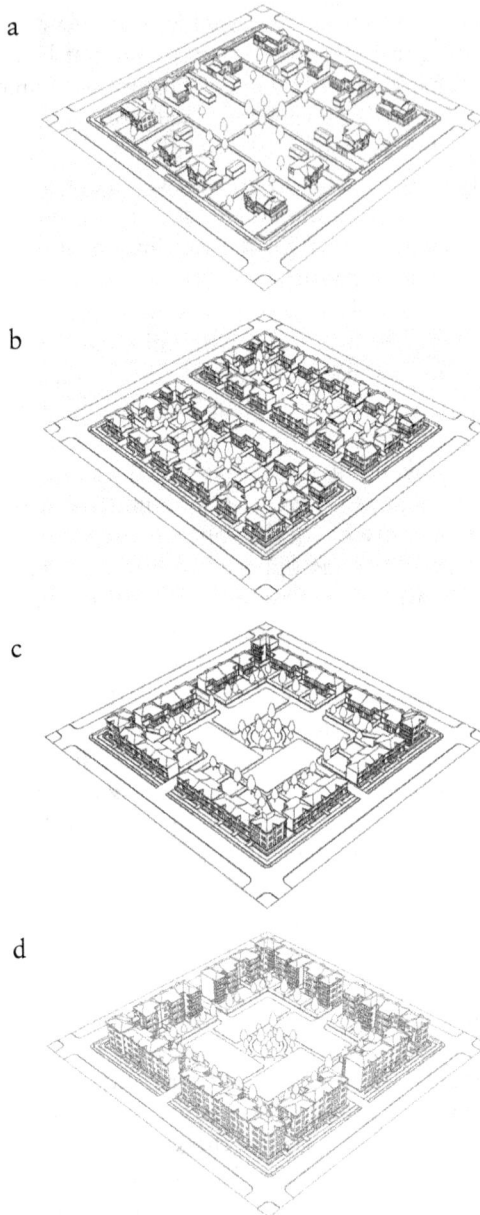

Figure 8.5 A diagrammatic representation of residential layouts at varying density levels based on a 100 m × 100 m perimeter block matrix. (a) Detached houses at 15 dph. (b) The block is divided into two 50 m × 100 m blocks with terraced houses used to obtain a density of 30 dph. (c) Flats are used to turn the corners of a 100 m × 100 m block to raise the density to approximately 50 dph. (d) Flats are used throughout, raising the density to 100–120 dph

Source: Drawn by Matthew Ryan under the direction of the author © Tony Hall

throughout, but with a maximum height of four storeys and with communal gardens, raises the density to 100–120 dph. Note that this can be achieved without recourse to underground or multi-level car parking and within a height of four storeys, thus keeping both embodied and operational energy use within bounds. The important point here is not just the maintaining of the original grid of streets, not just the use of perimeter block form but the maintaining of un-built areas within the blocks. This allows for a range of design solutions that enables the parking of motor vehicles to be effectively managed and, most importantly, to retain private green space for the dwellings. However, this *robust* approach should not be confined to the layout within the blocks but should be designed in concert with open space and other planning considerations leading to the morphological and *character area* formulation set out in the previous section.

Redevelopment of existing residential areas

The locational criteria developed in the previous chapters as a basis for the theoretical model can then be used to guide the location of areas of increased intensity within existing residential areas. Ped-sheds can be drawn around selected stations on existing quality public transport lines within existing urban areas. Having regard to terrain and other planning considerations, such as age and quality of existing roads and buildings, some ped-sheds could be selected for intensification with the density being related to the distance from the public transport station. Retail, commercial and community uses would be encouraged around the station to create or consolidate a local centre. The areas equivalent to the green enclaves in the theoretical model, that is, the areas beyond the ped-sheds, would remain at their existing density level and would be protected by planning policy from intensification. The suitability of existing residential areas for intensification could be changed by building new quality public transport facilities, for example street-running light rail or underground heavy rail, through the existing suburbs, creating new station stops that could act as a focus for intensification.

Figure 8.6 shows a diagrammatic representation of the application of the theoretical model to the residential intensification ofr an existing urban area. The railway station could be existing or proposed. As examples, levels one to three represent increasing degrees of intensification and could be expressed as morphological and character areas as discussed previously. The actual quantities could vary according to local circumstances and policies. For example, the existing density level might be 20 dph, level one 30 dph, level two 50 dph and level three 100 dph. However, it is the method rather than the actual values that is being stressed here. What we have is a practical method for handling the design and location of areas of increased residential intensity. This is not to say that intensification is automatically a *good thing* or a *bad thing* but rather to show how it could be the subject of a rational planning policy.

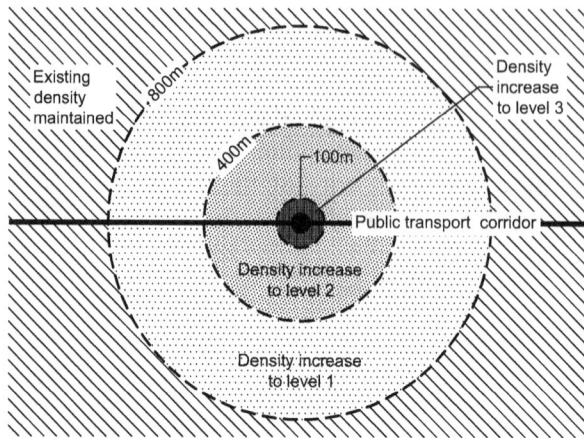

Figure 8.6 A diagrammatic representation of the application of the theoretical model to the residential intensification of an existing urban area. As examples, levels one to three represent increasing residential densities and the quantities could vary according to local circumstances and policies. The railway station could be existing or proposed

Source: Drawn by Matthew Ryan under the direction of the author. © Tony Hall.

Summary

This chapter has shown how the lessons from the theoretical model developed in Chapters 6 and 7 can have application in practice, in particular to the extension and intensification of urban areas. What is provided is a more rational basis for planning which is assisted through providing a systematic stepwise approach to the design of development. It provides, in effect, a practical tool kit as well as an intellectual justification. It does this, in essentials, by stressing the importance of providing quality public transport routes and leaving green spaces between development at all levels of spatial resolution – urban tissues, intensified areas, urban extensions and agglomerations of cities.

References

Amati, Marco (2008) Green Belts: A Twentieth-century Planning Experiment, in *Urban Green Belts in the Twenty-First Century*, edited by M. Amati, Aldershot: Ashgate, pp. 1–17.

Buxton, Michael and Goodman, Robin (2008) Protecting Melbourne's Green Wedges – Fate of a Public Policy, in *Urban Green Belts in the Twenty-First Century*, edited by M. Amati, Aldershot: Ashgate, pp. 61–82.

Hall, A. C. (1996) *Design Control: Towards a New Approach*, Oxford: Butterworth-Heinemann.

Hall, A. C. (1997) Dealing with Incremental Change: An Application of Urban Morphology to Design Control, *Journal of Urban Design*, 2(3), pp. 209–227.

Hall, Tony (2007) *Turning a Town Around: A Pro-active Approach to Urban Design*, Oxford: Blackwell.

Hall, Tony (2008) The Form-based Development Plan: Bridging the Gap Between Theory and Practice in Urban Morphology, *Urban Morphology,* 12(2), pp. 77–96.

Unwin, Raymond (2013) *Nothing Gained by Overcrowding,* reprint of the 1912 pamphlet for the Garden Cities and Town Planning Association with an introduction by Mervyn Miller, Studies in International Planning History, Abingdon: Routledge.

9 Implications for development plans

What have the considerations advanced in this book to say on the procedural aspects of planning practice, in particular the nature of development plans? An immediate problem in considering this question is the number of different planning systems around the world. Those in North America are different in fundamental ways from the discretionary system in Britain, and other European countries are different again, and so again across other parts of the world. Furthermore, they can, and do, change over time. Obviously, there is no space here to describe, compare and review all these different approaches. What will be done is to select some particular aspects of development plans and to discuss their limitations in the light of the arguments advanced in this book in the hope that their correspondence with issues in practice will be recognised. Some positive proposals for an improved approach can then be made.

From the perspective of the arguments pursued in the previous chapters, there are a number of serious inadequacies that may limit the effectiveness of development plans. It is not suggested that they are present in all plan formats throughout the world at the time of writing. If readers find that the limitations do not apply to their own practice or, if they did in the past, that they have moved away from them, then this is good news. Nevertheless, it is important that they be considered, if only that the arguments for the best practice can be made clear. The topics for discussion will be the two-dimensional land-use allocation paradigm, the use of codes in plans, and the use of growth boundaries in plans and consistency between plan periods.

There will not be a lengthy and detailed examination of examples of plans around the world, past and present, in order to substantiate the criticisms. This could be done, but it would take up much space and would detract from the tone and purpose of the book, which is to be positive and make practical and useful proposals, rather than spend a lot of time and effort criticising. Hopefully, readers will find the emphasis on analysis and recommendations rather than on criticisms of actual examples more useful.

Limitations of the two-dimensional land-use allocation paradigm

The need for a new paradigm for local development plans can be argued wherever the format is constrained by thinking in terms of two-dimensional, uniform land-use allocations (Hall, 2000). As in previous chapters, *use* here refers to activities upon the land, such as residence, employment, shopping, recreation, education, rather than the built form. Basing development plans on uniform land-use parcels on a two-dimensional map to describe existing and desired land uses, and to propose locations for new development, has serious flaws. It is not just limiting but can, in some cases, cause thinking to be misdirected. It is increasingly inadequate for modern requirements.

It is not suggested that all such development plans are wholly map-based. Clearly, they may incorporate planning principles that are not directly spatial in character. However, there is a problem where a two-dimensional land-use paradigm is the predominant thinking behind such plans. What can be especially noticeable are the paucity of references to existing physical form and the absence of explicit three-dimensional proposals. It is as though land-use preferences are the basic structures on which policies are hung, with the characteristics of the physical form of development being a matter to be handled at a later stage of the process. This makes it an inadequate tool for achieving a more compact, sustainable form involving a mix of land uses. It limits its usefulness in negotiations and for the control of urban design.

The format of the plan as fundamentally a map allocating such activities to two-dimensional land parcels has a long history, whether or not it is the case everywhere now. Also, it must be said, in fairness to practitioners in the past, that the fact that governments and legal structures may have required plans in this format did not necessarily mean that all planners necessarily thought in these terms. Nevertheless, some undoubtedly did think in this way, to the extent that it affected their mode of thinking and could justifiably be referred to as a paradigm. Even though it may have been superseded in some quarters, it is important to understand thoroughly what its limitations were.

It will be argued that a particular limitation relates to dealing with urban design issues and mixed-use proposals. What is also missing is a way of controlling design and realising the outcomes of urban design policies and principles. Indeed, the land-use bias can actually obstruct many urban design goals. It also is an inadequate basis for public participation. Detailed physical proposals are a matter of concern to the lay public and are usually their point of contact with wider planning issues. Moreover, all these deficiencies obstruct the pursuit of a more compact and sustainable settlement design.

Problems in dealing with mix of use

Achieving a mix of uses is implied by the pursuit of goals of sustainability and quality of life as argued in the previous chapters. In a more compact and intensified urban form, the land uses will inevitably tend to be close together and to overlay in three dimensions. Granted, the lack of precision in the concept in practice can be worrying. What mixtures are desirable and in what proportions? These quantities can be, in reality, more important than whether or not there is a mix at all. However, what is unavoidable is the need for development plans to deal explicitly with mix of use and with these associated questions.

What concerns us here is whether development plan formats help or hinder achievement of sustainable form. Clearly, they do not allow for it if they actually inhibit a mix of uses by adopting uniform land-use notations. A further inhibition is the lack of a three-dimensional land-use notation. Plans have to deal with changes of use within existing structures as well as guiding new building. In city centres, changes can take place in three dimensions. For example, development can mean the subdivision of dwellings or the change of use of flats over shops to offices. Housing and offices overlaying other uses, however, cannot be shown. Another example is that local shops within housing areas must either be shown as very small separate land uses in precise locations, allowed for as part of a general policy provision for residential areas, or seen as an exception to policy.

It could be argued that it is the commercial development process that produces the parcels of uniform land use as a result of the pressure of market forces. However, it could be countered that whereas it is indeed in the interests of the financial backers of developers, it does not reflect the demands of end-users. On the contrary, the real pattern of demand, particularly by smaller concerns, may only be facilitated by the intervention of the planning process to ensure the provision of smaller size offices, houses and other uses. The intervention of the planning system could have the effect of realising the demand for a mix of uses in three dimensions. A two-dimensional uniform land-use approach reinforces the desire of property developers to partition sites for sale as different uses rather than achieve a closely related mix.

Problems in dealing with urban design

What are the inadequacies of the paradigm for achieving quality in urban design? Take first the concern of urban design for the spaces defined by buildings. The use of uniform land-use notations can be seen not only to have little provision for this but also to actually cause problems. The boundaries of land uses are frequently drawn along the lines of roads, rivers and railways. Yet roads and rivers are urban spaces defined by buildings that should be designed as a whole. Different policies for each side of the street or each river bank can cause obvious dislocation. Similarly, parks on a land-use map will have their perimeters defined by the edge of the public open space. For urban design purposes they should be seen as spaces defined by the surrounding buildings and the combination should be planned as a whole.

Take next the elements of form from which town space is composed, such as streets, squares and building types. A land-use map gives little guidance. Without some indication of block structure, issues of permeability and legibility cannot be dealt with. Furthermore, the land-use map does not indicate those elements of the form of urban and rural areas that might be permanent as opposed to those that might be liable to change. This is a limiting factor in its effectiveness as a controlling mechanism. It also makes it difficult to deal with matters of urban history. Some elements of form, such as plot boundaries, tend to be resistant to change for legal reasons, while retained as a political decision because of their value to the community. It is from these ideas that concepts of conservation and character, clearly popular with the public, arise.

Problems in dealing with negotiation and participation

A two-dimensional land-use plan format may be useful for dealing with some general debates, for example on the location of significant new parcels of greenfield development or the line of a major road proposal. However, it is less so for more detailed matters. The absence of proposals on physical form means that the residents of a neighbourhood get no chance to engage in debates on its future form or style. Should it be conserved? Should there be infill or backland development? Instead of the matter being debated with alternatives displayed, the initiative passes to the developer and it is the developer's proposal that is considered by the planning authority with the residents being put in the position of objectors. No full discussion of alternatives takes place.

It is often objected that a more detailed and prescriptive stance by a planning authority would cramp the style of developers and prevent imaginative options being considered. It would be unpopular with them. However, this would not necessarily be the case. It is uncommon for major developers to be experimental. They seek success in business and their proposals are driven by the market forces within which they find themselves. What they want is certainty, and certainty early on in the process. Knowing at an early stage in the process what is likely to be approved in some detail can save a lot of money. Moreover, they would be able to make their representations if, and when, public participation on the plan content takes place.

The underlying problem is that the actual, as opposed to very general, goals and objectives are not made clear by the plan. Negotiations work best if each side makes clear what are their essential requirements as opposed to what is open for compromise or even suggestion. Deducing plan content from goals in a detailed and prescriptive manner can, therefore, aid and reinforce the process of negotiation.

The use of codes in plans

In addition to, or even instead of, land-use allocations, development plans may incorporate *codes* that specify what is allowed, and what is not allowed, regarding buildings and other structures in three dimensions. These may include, for example, maximum building heights and distances between buildings and highways. In some parts of the world, they have a quite long history. A common problem with them is that both their parameters and the actual numerical values specified for them may not be linked directly to planning goals, even where goals have been specified. In many cases, there may be a specific quantity for, say, maximum height but no clear representation of how this quantity forms part of the overall vision for the design of the area in question, nor how it relates to the other parameters used and the numerical values specified for them. In some cases this may be because there are no clear goals specified in the plan, because the goals are just *motherhood* statements lacking in direct physical consequences. Even when there are fairly specific goals and local objectives in the plan, just how the choice of parameters and their numerical values were derived may not be clearly articulated. In the worst case, the links may not be apparent at all.

The first decades of the twenty-first century have seen the production, by some planning authorities in different parts of the world, of *design codes* or *form-based codes*. These have attempted to remedy the deficiencies referred to by making clear the outcomes for the design of the physical form of selected urban areas and the way that the particular codes help to achieve this. This is not to say that they are always entirely successful in meeting the challenge but the fact that they needed to be created does serve to illustrate the nature of the problem. It is suggested here that the argument of the previous chapters can provide a method for generating the articulation needed for such *design codes* and *form-based codes*, that is, goals clearly linked to physical form leading to locational criteria, and all the way to the implementation of the desired physical form. It could also provide a method for assessing the merits of particular development plans and the extent to which the codes that they may contain were genuinely *design* or *form* based.

Limitations of the use of growth boundaries in plans

In Chapter 8, the relationship of the proposals in previous chapters to the planning device known as the *green belt* was discussed. The same arguments can be applied to the policy and planning instrument known as the *urban growth boundary*, which has great similarities, if not complete equivalence. Under this name, it had its origin in the state of Oregon, USA, and subsequently migrated to parts of Australia and also to other countries. Within a development plan for a city region, a limit is shown on a map beyond which urban expansion would not be allowed. Predicted growth must take place within this spatial boundary. It must be pointed out immediately that there is nothing wrong in principle with specifying within a plan areas where development would not, perhaps would never, be permitted, and also for such land areas, where appropriate, to be very extensive. Planning is about saying where development should, and should not, go and there will always be some places where it should never go. As was explained in Chapter 8, British planning, for example, has always routinely made such statements at all spatial levels. Indeed, a *green belt* can put very large areas out of bounds to urban expansion. It is possible to argue that it was the general lack, for quite significant legal and political reasons, of such policies in American planning that gave rise to the need for the urban growth boundaries in Oregon and, subsequently, elsewhere.

The problem that we have is not in the principle but in the spatial detail, that is, where do you draw the line? This can be very important at a local level to people whose property is affected, but development plans across the world rarely address it – there is no direct coupling with the goals and objectives or, at least, none that is made explicit. In the absence of some obvious physical barrier, there is no criterion that is used to clearly demarcate the boundary line. At any particular location, it is possible that a lot of thought has gone into the matter behind the scenes and that a lot of evidence has been considered at the detailed level. However, this is rarely made explicit and the suspicion grows that there is much intuition, subjectivity and, in the worst cases, arbitrariness. This is also the problem relating to infrastructure. Infrastructure may be seen as something that can only be planned in detail over shorter time periods depending on financial and other political considerations. However, growth depends on infrastructure and how, therefore, can a properly planned long-term boundary be determined if long-term infrastructure is not also determined? The implication is that infrastructure is not seen as a central consideration – in effect, a *non-plan* position.

One significant difference between the concept of the green belt and that of the growth boundary is that much of the debate around the green belt centres on the use of the land within, whereas the debate on the growth boundary focuses on the effect on the urban area it contains, in particular its implications for increases in residential density. This occurs in part because the land beyond the green belt in Britain is much more highly urbanised, and experiences much higher development pressures than in the hinterland of many large cities in western North America, where low-density suburbs expand into largely undeveloped areas. The argument of this book, however, takes another tack entirely. As was argued in Chapter 3, it is unwise to assume that the city will not continue to grow either outwards or that its density will not increase and this growth must be planned for. Although it is entirely appropriate for plans to say where development should not go, green belts and growth boundaries are, at best, blunt instruments and, at worst, inadequate policies. This book attempts to show a better way.

Lack of consistency between plan periods

Even when development plans do address physical form in a comprehensive manner, there is still the issue of the *plan period*, the time period during which the policies of the development plan will apply and, hopefully, be enforced. Unfortunately, there is often little evidence around the world of consistency in approach to the location and design of development between plan periods. Each successive plan period may not only present different policies but they may be based on different ideas and even different goals. Using the terminology set out at the beginning of Chapter 4, new *objectives* are to be expected in each period but changes to the basic values and principles will be problematic, given the long-term nature of the built form. However, additional goals may not necessarily be an issue. As has been argued in the previous chapters, adding *pursuit of sustainability* goals to *pursuit of quality of life* goals over the decades has reinforced, rather than changed, the pattern of goals and their consequences.

The common problem is not really one of changing goals but of the weak articulation between goals, local objectives and with the implementation of particular designs and layout of built form. Where the link is weak, as it usually is, then there is a lack of integration between the plan periods. There is also a failure to recognise the persistence of form, as argued in Chapter 1, that is, the development implemented in one plan period will last for many. On top of this, there is the apparent belief that each extension of the city will be the last – there is no plan for continual expansion. As argued in Chapter 3, this can result in physical discontinuities in the urban form and consequent difficulties in extending infrastructure provision. What is needed is a recognition that, although much will change between plan periods, there should be specific plan content that does not. As explained in Chapter 4, there are goals, criteria and design qualities that can be expected to endure and which all have physical consequences. For example, if habitats and buildings are to be retained because of their heritage value, then these values must last indefinitely if the policy is not to become a nonsense. Similarly, if it is considered important that people should be able to access facilities within walking distance of where they live, then it is not clear why this should change between plan periods. If it did change, then the long-term physical consequences would be disruptive. An analogy can be made here with the constitution of a country or of an organisation. Although laws and policies may change and develop over time, the constitution itself should be very difficult to amend and thus remain a constant and stabilising feature. Note that constitutions of countries are usually value-laden documents, promoting particular individual and political rights, and are not just a collection of rules and procedures. (The American constitution is a particular case in point.) In the same way, a development plan should contain values that will be passed on to the next, and subsequent, plan periods. These values should be linked strongly to locational criteria for development that, recognising the long-term persistence of physical form, ensures continuity of its basic structure over time as the city expands.

The proposed approach

Implications of the theoretical model

What the theoretical model shows us is that it is possible to derive the physical structure of city regions from explicit criteria which can endure over very long time periods. It shows clearly how they distinguish between areas where development is permitted and areas where it is not. This may appear to suggest that, even at regional and sub-regional levels, a development plan should specify the location of built-up areas and infrastructure over a very wide area for a timescale of many decades, if not centuries. Surely, the reader will object; this is unrealistic, to put it mildly. However, this is not what the theoretical model and the other arguments of this book imply.

A development plan for a robust city region over a very long time period would not, necessarily, be deterministic and based upon detailed two- and three-dimensional designs, conveyed pictorially. What it would have is a close coupling between the objectives, criteria and planning decisions governing the location of buildings and infrastructure. It would consist of strong and explicit criteria that were directly derived from similarly explicit goals. The arguments would also apply to intensification of development. Achieving higher density of use is not something that the conventional development plan, in particular the map content, can easily deal with for exactly equivalent reasons. There is an apparent paradox here. Planning for the construction of urban form over a long time period may not necessarily require a detailed master plan. Instead, the pattern of form could be determined by locational criteria strongly linked to the goals. Such criteria will not, in themselves, ensure that desirable urban activities take place but they will require built form that will not prohibit such activities in the long term. Other planning policies will deal with the actual nature and promotion of the desired activities in the shorter term.

The point was made in Chapter 1 that a decision on, say, the erection of a building made at a particular point in time is, in effect, a long-term one in relation to physical form. How incremental change in physical form is handled is, therefore, of paramount importance (Hall, 1997). A plan is not just about major new developments but also about guiding incremental change taking place through a multitude of decisions on smaller matters. It is here that a plan based on physical form, and not just land use, is really required. It needs to be supplemented by other planning instruments and these instruments need to have an explicit relationship with physical form. They need to take on a more holistic view of urban form, as opposed to specification of a limited number of parameters. In recent years, changes have been afoot in many countries around the world that would permit this. As discussed in the section on planning codes above, where codes are used there have been moves to ones that are explicitly *design codes* or *form-based codes*. In the more open, discretionary style of the British system, *design guides* and *site-specific briefs*, which have a long history, have, over recent decades, become increasingly clear on the desired patterns of physical form. Under all systems, *master plans* for imminent major developments are now increasingly common. What is argued here is that they should fit within a rationally based development plan structure.

The problem in all these matters is not thinking them – others have already done so – but doing so in a way that makes them a reality. What the model shows is that the long-term locational criteria can be as universal as the goals of *pursuit of sustainability* and *pursuit of quality of life* from which they are derived. Their application will vary according, say, to terrain but not the criteria themselves. In particular, the model leads to a set way of planning urban extensions and managing urban intensification, providing both a stepwise procedure and guidance on content.

A new format for development plans

To try to turn these ideas into a new format for development plans, the argument must start by dealing with what a development plan should be. The plan should be seen as a published output of a process of policy development. The underlying assumptions should be that this process:

* is there to achieve something;
* involves negotiation within a pluralist social context.

The published statement is not the whole process but is an essential part of this process. The whole process is something which is ongoing and evolving. It must embody the process even though it is only part of it. Negotiation requires the use of published statements, and their design is important for the effectiveness of the process. This may appear paradoxical, but it is the tension that is inherent in this paradox that is at the heart of all debate about the nature of development plans.

A long-term, goal-derived, criteria- and objective-driven plan can also be used to identify and assess specific, shorter-term planning problems, another apparent paradox. The reason for this is that the specific issues arise because of the mismatch between goals and objectives and the actuality on the ground. The pursuit of a solution to them can, therefore, be greatly assisted by clarity about the intentions and the pursuit of such clarity should be an important part of the policy development process. This will be aided by and, indeed, may necessitate, an issues-based, rather than topic-based, plan format. A topic-based format, whereby a plan is structured under standard headings of population, employment, housing, recreation, education, encourages a checklist approach which discourages perception of the underlying goals and objectives.

The goals and objectives should be used to generate strategic criteria that will guide the location and form of development over long plan periods, say 20 to 30 years, and beyond. They would constitute the first stage of a development plan. These would, in turn, be used to generate more detailed criteria for a locational structure within the plan on which to base objectives for parts of the plan area, and the smaller areas within these component parts. The development plan goals and criteria that relate directly to physical form should be seen as the key ones. Their interaction with the existing form can be used to produce local objectives and local policy areas based upon them. From these local objectives would be deduced the detailed proposals for development (Hall, 2008).

This does not imply that all parts of the plan area should be provided with a detailed physical structure. There is the matter of time period and a matter of degree of specificity. Detailed physical guidance in two and three dimensions will be required for those sites where development is close at hand in time. In addition, the degree of detail can be adjusted to both the time period concerned and the likelihood that the development will take place. Different physical options can be generated depending upon the degree of intervention proposed. For example, how much does a plan permit or encourage change? It can be argued that these degrees of intervention are equivalent to degrees in change in urban form over time (Hall, 1997). Morphological techniques developed for analysis of change over time can, therefore, be used to describe the alternative objectives for the design of localities. The result would be a range of alternative objectives for the physical form of small areas that could be shared with the public and their views sought. The resulting plan would contain a map dividing up the plan area according to desired or existing physical form. The degree of intervention for each of the component parts would be reflected in the amount of physical detail shown. More general land-use policy and proposals would, of course, still be present but they would be structured in a different way.

Dealing with complexity

It would no doubt be said that introducing more emphasis on elements of physical form into plans in the manner described would add to their complexity. They would, in consequence, take even longer to prepare and approve than they do at present. Against this, it can be argued that complexity in plans is essential if they are to be effective. Complexity is already present in current planning decision making. The proposal here is that the inevitable complexity of a development plan and the policies guiding it should be made more explicit. Paradoxically, this would make it more accessible to the public and would give more certainty to developers. The conclusion drawn is that plans must, inevitably, be complex documents.

There is a problem here. The human mind likes to simplify in order to understand. A policy document that deals only with a limited number of options can be useful for teaching and learning but it is restricted in its use for other purposes. It is no good as a control mechanism. This takes us to the subject of cybernetics and Ashby's *law of requisite variety* (Ashby, 1956). To control a system the controlling mechanism must be able to exist in as many states as that being controlled. A very simple device cannot control a complex phenomenon, only a limited part of it. The tension between the desire for *simple*, and therefore *speedy*, procedures and plans and the need to control complex phenomena is very evident in the history of town and country planning in many parts of the world.

What is being argued is that development plans must, of their very nature, be complex documents, as they have to be a means of controlling complex situations. Much of this is a matter of how plans are designed and put together. They do not have to be incomprehensible, neither do they have to be rigid. On the contrary, rigidity is the reverse of sophistication. The misconception is often that complexity means detail. What it should mean is *details linked to criteria* rather than *details as free-standing items*. Planning criteria should form the essential structure of any policy document and in a local plan they are vital. It is the *why* of where development should be located that is more important than the precise locational outcome, although both may be needed.

The processes of the plan should be clearly understood. The detail will appear highly complex and, indeed, will be highly complex. The important point is that it should readily respond almost organically to changing and intricate political circumstances. It can only do this if it is clear on what may be liable to change and what may be more robust over time.

Aiding negotiation with developers and other stakeholders

A greater emphasis on physical form through the use of locational criteria and more physically conceived local objectives would aid, rather than obstruct, local negotiations through greater transparency of intention on the part of the planning authority. This transparency is an essential part of the involvement of the public and the negotiation with developers. Development plan production and incremental control, although separated out organisationally in most parts of the world, are in reality different aspects of the same process. Firstly, as policy is being implemented, there must exist a conception of policy. Even if it is not written down, there will be an image in the mind of the planning officer. This may be a matter of degree. If only the bare bones are put down on paper then a lot is left to the thought process. It is often argued that it is right to leave a lot of scope to the developer. This is, in reality, an argument about the actors in the process: a discussion of who does what. The problem with this line of thinking is that, when taken to extremes, it can represent an abdication of what planning is intended to achieve.

Whatever the methods and thought processes that are deployed within the planning process, its outcomes must be physical and the quality of the physical form is the ultimate test in the eyes of the public. This is why what is being proposed here should be seen as a paradigm shift. It accepts that the way plans are prepared does, in itself, reveal assumed values. Nothing in town and country planning is value free. It emphasises that physical form is important to people. It is the source of both the character of towns, especially where a sense of place provides joy and interest for people's lives, and also the more prosaic human requirements of feeling secure and being able to find the way. All parties to the development process ought to be talking the language of physical form at an early stage in their deliberations. It should be the starting point of the structuring of the discussions of planning policy at the local level. It is not being argued that this is the only thing that planning is about – far from it. In some parts of the world and at some points in the past this has indeed been argued and it is false. However, it is equally misconceived to think only of land use and to consign physical form to being a consequence rather than a prerequisite.

Language for expressing form

This leads on to the issue of the language in which the plan is expressed and whether this is adequate to convey the policies relating to physical form. Having a picture of the desired urban form is one thing; getting to it is another. If appropriate and precise language is used in both the planning instruments and negotiations then successful outcomes will be much more likely. One of the reasons why planning codes have not been *design* or *form* based in the past is that their authors have had difficulty in obtaining an adequate means of expressing how their choice of parameters of form relates to the achievement of the end product. Planning processes present similar challenges as they operate incrementally over long time periods and can involve negotiations between many stakeholders. Both lay and professional stakeholders may have difficulty appreciating the full physical implications of policy without an adequate language to express it.

This leads to a further and significant contribution that the study of urban morphology can make to the planning process. It can provide a language that conveys the essential components of the desired physical outcome by disaggregating the elements of which urban form is composed. In Chapter 1, the work of Conzen was discussed in relation to the issue of the persistence of different aspects of urban form over long time periods. His work also provides terminology and definitions for the description and analysis of urban form. Similar, and very important, work has been carried out by other scholars, notably Caniggia and Maffei, and it is possible to attempt a consistent formalisation of the definitions and concepts in this field (Kropf, 2014). For example, a compositional hierarchy could have the following levels:

- *building materials* which go to make up
- *structural elements* which go to make up
- *rooms* which go to make up
- *buildings* which are situated within
- *plots* which may be arranged to form
- *plot-series* which may go to form streets that, together with other elements, make up
- 'urban tissues' or 'plan-units'.

Rather than talking just about 'scale', it becomes possible to use the concepts of:

- the *level of resolution* whereby the properties apparent at the desired spatial scale are noted; and
- the *level of specificity,* whereby the degree of particularity used is defined.

Looking at a town at a low level of resolution, only the plot-series would be identified. Increasing the resolution results in greater specificity as the plots and then the buildings within the plots are identified. At each level of resolution different *types* can be identified. For example, the plot-series for a Georgian terrace is quite different from an inter-war suburban street. The different *types* can be distinguished by reference to the *position, outline* and *arrangement* of the elements that compose them.

What this type of terminology provides is a language for conveying desired form that, because of its precision, is responsive to degrees of intervention by a planning system. It makes it easier, and more effective, in relating the desired actions and interventions in the development process to plan objectives. It also assists in dealing with incremental change (Hall, 1997, 2000).

Can the plan be monitored and tested?

This interplay of the long- and short-term planning processes can be important for testing the proposals that have been made in this book. Some readers might object that some of the points made are just assertions. If we are talking about the very long term, how would we know that it actually works, that is, that the proposed pattern of form does obstruct some essential goals in ways not anticipated by this book? The answer is that the proposed form can be tested for *falsification* because the argument is that physical form should not obstruct the fulfilment of the desired goals (as opposed to promoting them). The language used here is taken by analogy from Popper's concept of falsification of hypotheses in the scientific method (Popper, 2002). This is not an analogy to be taken too far, or too literally. The author was brought up a scientist in his early days and is aware of the need to be careful here. However, one can say that the design of the physical form has been obtained from the goals in a deductive manner. Once built, its effects can be monitored to see whether the fulfilment of any of the goals is obstructed. Obstruction of the political, economic and social processes will become apparent in the shorter term. If this occurs, then the approach set out will be undermined. If it is not, it can be continued into the longer term. However, this is yet to happen. The modes of implementation in practice suggested in Chapter 8 have not yet occurred in any measurable scale. The examples are discussed in Chapters 6 and 7 but these correspond only to selected aspects of what is proposed here. Nevertheless, if the proposals set out in Chapter 8 were implemented then they could be monitored and tested within each plan period to see if the fulfilment of any of the goals has been obstructed.

Summary

The need for a new paradigm for development plans has been argued. Present paradigms are particularly constrained where they consist basically of two-dimensional uniform land-use allocations. This limits their usefulness in negotiations and for the control of urban design. They are an inadequate tool for achieving a more compact, sustainable form involving a mix of land uses. Principles on which a development plan should be conceived in terms of outlines of physical form in three dimensions have been proposed. They would be the primary consideration. Land-use allocations would still be an important matter, but secondary to the physical guidelines. The degree of physical detail shown would vary within the plan according to the implications of area-specific policies and their proximity in time. The result would be a complex document, and this complexity is necessary if planning goals are to be attained with an explicit sense of what is to be achieved, and the proposals made would enable the complexity to be properly handled, mainly through criteria-based approaches.

Development plans should make clear:

- the planning goals, locational criteria and local objectives;
- the relative persistence of physical form in relation to land use;
- those goals and locational criteria which will apply beyond the plan period.

The level of physical detail, and degree of intervention by the planning process, may vary across the plan area according to local context and imminence of development, but, where appropriate, the plan should:

- make clear which elements of existing physical form should be liable to change and which should remain as they are;
- guide the design of buildings, the spaces they create and enhance the public realm;
- facilitate the specification of mix of uses, especially in three dimensions.

Although what is being described and argued for is a new development plan format, the proposals have wider significance. The proposals made are not just for a new form of proposals map but for a different way of thinking about development plans and the management of development generally. Changing ways of thinking is a long-term matter and is never easy. The task will take many years to initiate, let alone complete. What can be done now is to set a new sense of direction.

References

Ashby, W. R. (1956) *An Introduction to Cybernetics*, London: Chapman Hall.

Hall, A. C. (1997) Dealing with Incremental Change: An Application of Urban Morphology to Design Control, *Journal of Urban Design,* 2(3), pp. 221–239.

Hall, A. C. (2000) A New Paradigm for Development Plans, *Urban Design International*, 5(2), pp. 123–140.

Hall, Tony (2008) The Form-based Development Plan: Bridging the Gap Between Theory and Practice in Urban Morphology, *Urban Morphology,* 12(2), pp. 77–96.

Kropf, Karl (2014) Ambiguity in the Definition of Built Form, *Urban Morphology,* 18(1), pp. 41–57.

Popper, Karl (2002) *Conjectures and Refutations: The Growth of Scientific Knowledge,* reprinted edition, London: Routledge.

Conclusion

We can now draw out the overall lessons and recommendations from the arguments of the previous chapters. What has been remarkable is how concepts of a different nature, namely the analysis of urban form and societal goals, can be brought together and how apparent paradoxes in the design of cities can be resolved. There have also been some unexpected, though beneficial, results.

The first chapter drew attention to the longevity of the physical form of urban areas – the street plan and buildings may last longer than the activities they support by a very wide margin. To plan for urban activities requires the recognition of these long-term physical requirements. This is especially so when dealing with the private motor vehicle, as was discussed in Chapter 2. As urban areas change over time, it becomes necessary to retrofit them by adapting buildings, by rebuilding them and by renewing and extending the infrastructure. This is especially the case where the city and city region experience prolonged expansion. Increases in residential density will require similar retrofitting. Chapter 3 observed that this expansion is the norm rather than the exception and that, at the very least, there is no basis for assuming that a city will never expand beyond its existing limits. If, therefore, a city is to be planned it must be *robust*: it should be designed to accommodate change, particularly the expansion of infrastructure, on a continual basis. In the long term, this is what matters for the planned city and *long term* can amount to many decades if not many centuries.

Although, at first sight, very long-term physical planning may seem like a tall order, it has been shown that it is perfectly feasible. It can be achieved by intervening rationally and systematically in the design of the physical form of new development. Chapters 4 and 5 showed that appropriate types of urban form could be derived, or deduced, from planning goals. The types and characteristics of form are the consequence of human behavioural goals and planned form has no meaning without them. The desired patterns of physical form can be deduced from two sets of goals – pursuit of quality of life and pursuit of sustainability. It must be stressed that it is not claimed that this would be a strictly causal or deterministic process. What is suggested is that types of form and their characteristics may arise from a convergence of goals achieved at the same location or may resolve potential conflicts between goals, resulting in favourable and optimal solutions.

Although there may be a variety of details in practice, there appears, fortunately, to be only a narrow range of general types consistent with the goals. There is no need to have to consider and evaluate an infinite variety of types and characteristics. As a bald statement, this may sound over-ambitious; there are reasons why it is much more realistic than it sounds. At a local level, both urban design practice and the theory that underpins it have evolved since the late 1970s in a way that has produced a remarkable convergence of built outcomes – shallow-plan buildings arranged in perimeter blocks on a grid type street pattern with an active public realm. A more pragmatic observation is that such arrangements have been shown to work throughout the historic periods before the twentieth century.

Some readers may have become concerned about what is not dealt with in this book. Surely, they may say, economic planning, especially regeneration, aesthetics and the creation of distinctive and attractive places, community planning and housing are all very important but have not been discussed in detail in terms of how they relate to the theoretical model. These matters certainly are vitally important and nothing in this book is intended to suggest otherwise. The argument here is that not only do buildings and infrastructure and their spatial layout last longer than the lengths of the cycles of economic and social change, but they provide a physical framework within which they occur. This physical framework may not necessarily determine, or even promote, socio-economic change in a causal sense but it can obstruct, or even prevent, desired outcomes. Its relationship to the creation of a sense of place and conservation of urban heritage is much more direct. This is why planning such a long-term framework is fundamental.

The robust city structure

What then would be the nature of the form of this robust city at the strategic level? There is nothing a priori to suggest that a general solution would exist but, fortuitously, one does. There is more to the matter than just the establishment that this is a rational and realistic path. The argument leads to locational principles that can provide a sufficient foundation for long-term physical planning. These locational principles can be used to generate a repeating pattern. It was argued in Chapter 6 that the key to generating robust, sustainable quality urban form is to adopt the planning principle that major development should be allowed only where it is possible to walk to a stop on a quality public transport line. This would create what are termed *ped-sheds*. A maximum radius of 800 m was proposed but the argument does not depend on the precise quantity.

The ped-sheds can be strung along a high-quality public transport line, normally track-based, to create a *beads-on-string* form. This is not an original idea and it has been suggested by a number of authors over a considerable time period and in a number of variants. What is original here was the way that it was used in Chapter 7 to construct a theoretical city model using a branching, radial pattern. Green spaces were left between the ped-sheds providing pedestrian access to land that offered opportunities for recreation and urban agriculture. Some ped-sheds could be wholly or partly non-residential and contain large health and educational complexes, commercial and industrial premises and park-and-ride facilities.

Some remarkable, and to a certain extent counter-intuitive, observations came out of the study of this model.

- The robust city does not require limits to growth placed around its periphery. It could, in theory, continue to expand without limit while still successfully pursuing quality of life and sustainability.
- This does not mean, however, that there are no limits on the extent of urban areas – far from it. What it means is that non-built-up areas or *green enclaves* would lie between the radial routes rather than being in the shape of *green belts* around the city. They would be similar to *green wedges* but would not necessarily be spatially open-ended, as a green wedge concept would normally be. What is important is that the shape and size of the green enclaves would not be arbitrary but a necessary and systematic consequence of the locational principles of development.
- The green enclaves would provide the space for the retrofitting of infrastructure.
- Although the locational principles are based completely and explicitly on facilitating walking and the use of public transport, the resulting city form would also permit, rather unexpectedly, almost unrestricted access by motor vehicles across the city. Motor vehicles would be severely restricted by speed within predominantly residential areas within the ped-sheds but would not encounter such restrictions when travelling between the ped-sheds through the green enclaves. They would be able to access park-and-ride facilities and commercial warehousing, distribution and manufacturing centres with little restriction.
- The same principles guiding the expanding structure of the city could also be applied to growing complexes of adjoining cities. They would be linked by transport corridors but separated by extensive green areas.

What is remarkable about the model is the advantageous implications of restricting development to within walking distance of public transport nodes. It results in quality movement about the city for motor vehicles as well, although such vehicles would have to accept significant speed restrictions within built-up areas. It permits the city to expand in a planned manner with room for the retrofitting of infrastructure within the existing boundary as the city grows. In more common parlance it allows the city to 'live and breathe' as it grows. The planned robust city appears to work perfectly.

Are cities really planned?

All this seems too good to be true. If it works so well why are not all cities planned this way? One answer to this question is that not all cities are really planned. In many parts of the world there will be planning legislation and procedures, there may be offices full of planning officers and planning decisions may be taken at the political level, but this does not necessarily imply that the content of the policies and their implementation is effective in controlling the city. In particular, for local political reasons, the planning intervention may have minimal impact on the actions of developers and, consequently, on the physical form, especially in the long term. However, even in those parts of the world where there is a strong political will to intervene in the design of new development there can still be limitations to the degree of actual planning. Even where a planning regime is very interventionist and has proper regard to the design of physical form in the long term, the argument of this book presents two significant challenges at the local political level.

- The first is the protection of the green enclaves. This is where the proposals made in this book appear at first sight to differ most markedly from actual city shape. However, as explained in Chapter 8, this may not be as large a challenge as might be supposed as long as policies for the proper protection and management of the natural environment are pursued.
- The second is the cost of providing quality public transport corridors at the same time as the new development it would serve. However, this challenge is not insuperable and can be overcome where planning mechanisms exist to recover the cost from within the development process through taxation of betterment, incorporation in the cost of the development or other means.

Overcoming these obstacles is, in effect, a necessary consequence of having a city that is genuinely planned. This is what a planned, as opposed to unplanned, city should be all about. The choice before us is between a city with a planning system and processes but which is not actually planned in any strategic sense and the planned and robust city as argued here.

Implications for planning practice

Implementation of the proposals made in this book does not necessarily require the construction of complete cities, and complexes of cities, on the lines of the theoretical model set out in Chapter 7. There are much more prosaic applications of the ideas that could be readily absorbed into day-to-day planning practice. As explained in Chapter 8, urban extensions can be designed using the beads-on-string form proposed and, indeed, a useful step-by-step method is available leading down from the strategic to local design criteria.

In addition, the ideas advanced can lead to a rational and stepwise method for planning the location of urban intensification. The proposals for the appropriate types of urban form also lead to a robust approach to residential layout, whereby future intensification is anticipated within its design. This rests, as with the city structure at large, on the maintenance of green areas both around and between buildings and within and between perimeter blocks. This not only fulfils an important range of environmental and recreational purposes but also facilitates any future intensification in a planned manner.

There are significant implications for the preparation of development plans in that the emphasis on physical form does not necessarily require the preparation of detailed master plans a long time in advance of development. Detailed two-dimensional maps and three-dimensional perspectives are essential for short-term planning but they are not required for the long term. This leads to at least an improved format, if not an entirely new paradigm, for development plans; a format that expresses the way that most urban activities take place within an enduring physical matrix of urban form. However, such plans do not need to set this form using an overly deterministic and detailed format but can use a formula or criteria-based approach for both the location of development and the expression of design qualities, with physical detail shown only where and when required. These criteria could then be carried over from one plan period to another to achieve long-term physical consistency.

The essential argument

The particular focus of the argument of this book is the physical structure of urban areas in the very long term from many decades to several centuries. Why? – because this is how long buildings and infrastructure last and it is difficult and expensive to keep rebuilding them. Without rebuilding, it can constrain or even prohibit specific urban activities and prevent them coming into close juxtaposition when this is thought desirable.

Economic and social forces will change markedly in the long term and it is desirable that the physical structure should be designed to cope with these changes. Planning ahead is a way of dealing with uncertainty. We have to think ahead to anticipate possible changes and to allow for them. In terms of physical form, this is what we mean by it being *robust* – it can cope with change over a wide range of outcomes. This does not mean necessarily that the long-tem robust structure is *value free*. The argument of this book has gone to some lengths to show how it can be determined by values. What it does imply is that some value choices have to be long term in order to be sensible. Conservation of cultural heritage is an obvious example but so are pleasant and sociable surroundings and conservation of resources. What is argued here is that there needs to be long-term choices to make sense of city planning. There must be locational principles that carry on from one plan period to another.

The pattern of form prescribed in this book is not just robust when compared to the changes in urban activities and infrastructure but also to the goals from which it is derived. The proposed layout of the robust city will survive detailed changes to sub-goals. It will also survive variation in the values of the parameters of form that have been used, such as residential density, walking distance, separation between ped-sheds and spacing of public transport stops. Moreover, the goals set out here are not, in themselves, unusual and novel. They are, indeed, to be found in most of the writing on social and environmental matters. They do not embody any really new innovation in values in the context of most progressive thinking that prevails at the time of writing. Similarly, the urban design qualities described are to be found in most texts on planning and design. What is novel here is the suggestion that not only should the physical consequences of the goals and qualities be taken to their logical conclusion, but that these physical consequences should be strictly implemented through planning legislation and procedures. In particular, it is proposed that all essential infrastructure, in particular quality public transport lines, should be constructed at the outset and that development should not occur where it cannot be reached by a combination of walking and good public transport. Other consequences follow. The different goals and qualities discussed all have their implications for the design of urban form. What is remarkable and fortuitous is that all these design implications are not only compatible with each other but tend to reinforce each other and that the resulting pattern of form in aggregate is consistent with all of the goals and qualities.

This is not to argue that the pattern of form will, in itself, deliver and fulfil all the goals. Other political, economic and social processes will, over time, be more or less successful in doing so. It must be stressed again at this point that the emphasis of the argument of this book on the very long term does not imply that the shorter term (i.e. 5–20 years) environmental, economic and social processes, for example economic regeneration schemes, are not important, as they most certainly are. On the contrary, the need to pay attention to the long-term physical form of urban areas is to ensure that such processes are not obstructed. What, therefore, is being argued here is that the pattern of form does not obstruct the fulfilment of the goals and qualities. In contrast, this obstruction is only too real in the non-planned and semi-planned city. Urban activities all take place within a long-lasting physical framework and they may not be successful unless this point is properly understood. The overall challenge is the construction of a city that is robust, sustainable and offers a high quality of life. This book has shown that it can be done and it has shown how it can be done.

Index

For Product Safety Concerns and Information please contact our EU
representative GPSR@taylorandfrancis.com
Taylor & Francis Verlag GmbH, Kaufingerstraße 24, 80331 München, Germany

www.ingramcontent.com/pod-product-compliance
Lightning Source LLC
Chambersburg PA
CBHW050518280326
41932CB00014B/2370

9 781138 631403